Plants of Paradise

Tropical Horticulture

Robin Robinson

Robin Robinson
Key West Citizen Columnist
for the
Key West Garden Club

Published by Sora Publishing

Sora Publishing
1800 Atlantic Boulevard, A-405
Key West, Florida 33040
U.S.A.

sorapublishing@comcast.net

keywestgardenclub.com

Library of Congress Cataloging-in-Publication Data
Robinson, Robin 1943-
plants of paradise
tropical horticulture: key west garden club

ISBN 978-0-9765756-3-4
includes index

SAN 256-4157

Cover design by Nathalie Breakstone

Although reported in the historical literature and from other sources, the author makes no representation or claims as to the accuracy, usefulness or viability of the Native American and other health or food uses of the plants and their products described herein. Such descriptions are for historical and entertainment references only and for no other purpose. No suggestion is made, nor intended, for the use of any plants or their products not certified by properly qualified medical or government authority. The ingestion of any plant or its products not tested and certified by proper governmental authority such as the U.S. Food and Drug Administration or the U.S. Department of Agriculture may cause detrimental health effects, including serious illness and death. It is not recommended.

About the Author

Key West Garden Club's Robin Robinson, a Master Gardener, was previously a columnist for the Chicago Daily News. Her children's column, "Robin's World" ran for ten years in over a hundred papers nationally and was syndicated by Princeton Features. Her book, *Peeling the Onion: Reversing the Ravages of Stroke,* (www.sorapublishing.com) can be found on Amazon.com. This column is part of a series developed by the Key West Garden Club, 1100 Atlantic Ave. Key West, Florida 33040. (305) 294-3210. Visit www.keywestgardenclub.com

After Wilma destroyed the courtyard gardens at her condominium complex she decided to help with the re-planting but found that she knew little about the native plants that would survive the next hurricane. Thus began the job of self-education and study with experts. Writing the column for the Key West Citizen resulted in detailed study of many native plants.

Forward

This book is a compilation of columns that appeared in the Key West Citizen between March 2008 and August 2009. It is by no means a comprehensive listing of plants found in the Florida Keys, but does include many natives and exotics that are commonly planted here, the only sub-tropical environment in the continental US.

I want to thank the Key West Garden Club for providing me with ideas and expertise and for sponsoring this column.

Table of Contents

Palms

Buccaneer Palm (*Pseudophoenix sargentii*)

Stately Buccaneer Palm Requires Patience to Grow

      The rarest of the twelve palms that are native to the Florida Keys is the buccaneer palm. It is not grown often in landscape nurseries because it grows only one leaf each year and takes ten years to turn into anything saleable. Because of that, it is expensive. I recently saw a six-foot tall specimen at Sears for $210, but you can have it free if you are patient and you grow your own.

      When the palm is full grown at about twelve feet in height, its bulging and constricted trunk is a swollen and waxy, green. It is easy to identify the palm because there are light brown rings around the pale green trunk. Leathery, pinnate fronds that are dark green on the top and silver underneath are standouts in the lush landscape. Don't confuse it with the Christmas palm that has similar red seeds.

The juvenile growth habit produces leaves in a single plane until the palm grows a trunk. After that, they form in a radius around the bud. Each new leaf is significantly larger than the last one. The palm is pest-free, but cold damages it, and therefore they do well in freeze-free Key West.

The buccaneer is an endangered native. It is drought, salt and wind tolerant and grows in well-drained, nutrient-poor soils. It can be planted near the ocean and thrives in alkaline soil. It is native only to a small area of the Keys, Cuba, Hispaniola, the Bahamas and Eastern Mexico.

A group of scientists studied four stands of the buccaneer palm in Dominica. They found the tallest to be fourteen and a half feet high and eleven inches in diameter. The oldest of the 3,340 palms they found was six inches in diameter and nine feet seven inches tall. It had 113 leaf scars which meant that it may be 113 years old. They named it Pampo after Elizabeth Pampo Israel, who is Dominica's oldest person at 127.

Bee-attracting, white inflorescence occurs in early winter, with green seeds beginning in January and ripe seeds available in February. The palm is sometimes called Sargent's cherry palm because the seeds look like bright red cherries.

Betrock's Guide to Landscape Palms by Alan W. Meerow, said that it is best to plant the seeds ASAP as they lose their viability quickly. At the Garden Club, everyone got a seed from Kitty Somerville's buccaneer palm. They wore gloves that had been sterilized with alcohol. They worked on a table top that also had been sterilized in order to remove the gooshy red outer flesh. Peeling off the white outer shell, they uncovered a garbanzo bean-sized endosperm. To find out if the seed was viable, they dropped the seed into water. If it sank it was viable, maybe.

Each gardener planted a seed ½ inch deep in containers sterilized with bleach and containing half perlite and half peat moss. If the planted seeds are kept damp and in the shade, they should germinate in two to four months.

In nature, the seed may dry out and float from island to island. Maybe that is why it is called the buccaneer palm as it sails off to different climes. The seed is so brightly colored it attracts wildlife, which can spread it around the Caribbean. In Dominica, scientists observed seeds being devoured by seed-eating birds like finches and woodpeckers. Lizards, rats and crabs also eat the seeds. I have a buccaneer palm beside the driveway that dropped its seeds under its branches and forty of them sprouted, so evidently it is fairly easy to sprout naturally. However, the Dominica scientists reported that when hurricanes hit, the seedlings were easily destroyed.

This is a good container palm as it grows so slowly it won't outgrow its pot or its space. In the ground, this is a no-trouble, stately collector's palm that other gardeners will stop to admire. It is a good test of the most difficult attribute to attain for a gardener--patience.

Cabbage Palm (*Sabal Palmetto*)

Cabbage Palm Is Dramatic and Useful

When transplanting a cabbage palm, all of the roots and leaves must be cut off. Almost all of them are transplanted from the wild as they are prolific seeders and it takes ten years before they are large enough—six feet--to transplant. Luckily, they transplant easily. What looks like a telephone pole is stuck in the ground and watered well. The trunk grows new roots and fronds as long as the central bud is not injured. Planting it in warm soil increases the palm's chance of survival. The state has planted thousands along the highway due to their resiliency.

This State of Florida symbol grows from North Carolina all the way around the Gulf of Mexico and up the west coast to Washington. It can take a freeze and weather a hurricane. It enthusiastically welcomes a drought or salt water or wind. It survives forest fires. If it grows in full sun, the tall trunk produces a tightly packed pom-pom of fronds that is fifteen feet in diameter on top of its fifty- to eighty-foot trunk. If it grows in the shade, the pom-pom is looser. Key West has planted *Sabal peregrima* in the Arecacea family, which grows to around twenty-five feet.

Fronds are costapalmate; costa means mid-rib. They look like they are doing a backbend, dividing in the center to send their leaves backwards into a half circle. Each frond can have up to ninety, dull, dark green blades. Their undersides are silver and they grow directly from the trunk without a crown shaft.

The weird thing about this palm is that on some trunks the leaf stem base falls off and on others it remains, forming criss-crossed boots that catch seeds from other plants which grow in the crevasses. A trunk can be covered with ferns or orchids and small animals often pop out unexpectedly. Young trunks feel rough and fibrous but will eventually age to silver smooth.

It will grow in almost any soil. Planted along beaches, in hardwood hammocks or city streets, this sturdy palm survives.

Creamy white flowers bloom in mid-summer, creating a beautiful inflorescence which turns into black seeds by fall and are devoured by the birds. It is the home of the cabbage palm caterpillar *(Litoprosopus futilis)* that can devour all of the inflorescence, thereby depriving Floridians of sweet palmetto honey.

The pink and black caterpillar will enter a home to pupate and it will use anything to make a cocoon: rugs, drapery, stuffed furniture, even fiberglass. Botanists have a hard time introducing predators because the caterpillar will regurgitate a material that is a self-defense against those predators. Eventually, it becomes the owlet moth, a two-inch, fawn colored creature with two black spots on its wingtips. The dead skirt on these palms also harbors beasties like cockroaches and rats so it should be removed, but not before it turns brown, as the palm re-absorbs the nutrients from the frond. Giant palm weevils can inflict damage, especially after transplanting. Ganoderma butt rot can enter if the trunk of the tree is injured. There is no cure for this disease.

Cabbage palm fronds were used by the Seminoles to roof their chickee hutch, hat their heads and sweep their floors. Panamanians use them to make Panama hats. Early settlers cut them down to use as logs for cabins, pilings for docks and hearts for their cabbage-like salad. Eating hearts of palm is frowned on now as companies are decimating Mexican and South American forests of *Sabal palmetto* in order to can them. Cutting the heart out, naturally, kills the palm.

For beauty and drama in a native, tropical landscape you can't beat the Cabbage Palm.

Cardboard Palm (*Zamia furfuracea*)

Cardboard Palm Is the Drama Queen of Your Garden

The drama queen of a tropical garden, cardboard palm, (*Zamia furfuracea*), bursts forth in profusion from a large storage root into a symmetrical rosette of hard, eight-foot tall branches. She is truly dramatic in a garden, but she needs a lot of space, like any true diva. She can easily dominate her stage and take over eight feet of space.

Although she's called a palm, that is only her stage name. Her real name should be cardboard cycad from the Zamiaceae family. *Zamia* from the Latin word meaning pine-nut and *furfuracea* means scruffy. She has a hard time getting started, with very slow growth the first two years until the trunk gets established. This trunk can be subterranean and up to ten inches in diameter and length and serves as a water reservoir in times of drought. Once she has herself established, she theatrically produces pale green limbs with soft, red, fuzzy leaves and begins to grow much faster. The leaves harden and turn dark green over time and sometimes develop a tooth on the tip and serrated edges. She has sharp fingernails.

If the spotlight is on her, she responds by pulling herself up to become erect in stature. If she is in the shade, she will lie horizontally. I can see her asking her owner to "Peel me a grape." She's been staging her own productions since before the dinosaurs. Her costumed leaf arrangement is spiral; her type is compound and oval.

When a cardboard palm goes to seed in the spring it is amazing. The male has a small dark rod that grows out of the center of the plant. A huge phallic seed cone grows, strangely enough, from the female plant. This seed cone ripens and bursts open, revealing about a hundred fire-engine red, plump seeds which fall to the ground under the leaves of their mother. These juicy red seeds have a good sprouting record, but like to be in the shade when they do. Their growth is painfully slow, with only two small leaves on the plant for the first year. The second year it may have three branches, but still looks scraggly. Finally, the new growth starts and the plant shoots up and out quickly.

Every part of this plant is poisonous. That is probably why they have survived and are called living fossils. The seeds are especially poisonous to dogs, that will eat them, and cats, who are usually more finicky. There is no known antidote.

Biologists are amazed that cardboard palms tolerate such a wide variety of conditions all over the world. These natives of Mexico are drought tolerant, wind and salt tolerant. Poor soil doesn't bother them a whit. They do like their environment to be well-drained and to be fed with palm food twice a year. This is an "outstanding plant and should be planted more often" according to the State of Florida. Plant collectors illegally harvest seedlings because they take so long to mature into anything that is saleable. The state considers it "vulnerable."

My experience with cardboard palms indicates that they will survive a hurricane, relying on the huge storage root and trunk to re-sprout leaves.

Plant the divine diva in a showy place in your garden and give her center stage with lots of room around her. She also pots well and would relish a starring role on your patio. You can get a small one for $16.95.

Silver palm *(Coccothrinax argentea)*

The Silver Palm Grows in a Biodiversity Hot Spot

The Arecaceae Family hosts the *Coccothrinax* genus with more than fifty species, generally called silver palm because the bottom of their leaves is silver. The *Coccothrinax argentata* is a slow-growing, slender palm first categorized by the famous botanist Carolus Linnaeus as *Principes* or the Prince of Palms. It graces our gardens with palmate (like your hand) silver fronds flashing in the sunlight. Its thin but regal height can reach twenty-five feet but most often is ten feet making it ideal for positions around a home, as it will not overpower the architecture.

The Prince is native to Key West which means that he has lived here thousands of years and has developed symbiotic relationships with beetles, bees, wasps and bats. He is a co-dependant part of the eco-system. Animals play a large part in the dispersal of his seeds.

The *Coccothrinax* genus was one of the first flowering plants. Evidence has been found in digs of the Late Cretaceous period eighty-five million years ago when Godwana was drifting apart to eventually form the present day continents. It is found throughout the Caribbean, the Bahamas, Southeastern Mexico and Southern Florida. However, most of the known species are only from

Cuba. Centering a visit to Cuba on identifying varieties of *Coccothrinax* would be a fascinating challenge. This patriot Prince is found in open habitats where the soil is sand or limestone. He doesn't mind salty wind or soil. His reign has no known enemies to undermine his rule.

The trunk of the *Coccothrinax argentata* is initially covered with fibrous leaf sheaths which eventually fall off, turning the stem into a smooth trunk. This fan palm is also called *guanito*, *guano*, broom palm and *cana*.

The bi-sexual white flowers bloom on short stalks. They seem to quiver because there are so many insects flying around them for their nectar. They attract the monk skipper butterfly *(asbolis capucinus)*. They turn into deep purple seeds that have a split, like the two parts of the brain. The birds go crazy over the seeds. *Coccus* means berry. *Argentata* means silver.

The dark blue leaves are used by traditional healers to treat uterine fibroids and hot flashes. Young leaves can be eaten as a vegetable. That does not mean that they taste good, it means that they won't kill you. Natives used them to make hats and baskets. The three-foot leaves are deeply divided and droop.

Take a trip to Bahia Honda State Park and you will be able to walk the beautiful Silver Palm Trail where there is one of the largest concentrations of palms in the state. The park brochure says that people illegally harvest this palm tree, removing it from its habitat and planting it in residential areas, so it is rare to see one in the wild. The U. S. Department of Agriculture has labeled it threatened.

It would do well planted in an above-ground planter as well as lining the roads or as a specimen plant. It likes part shade or full sun. Growing quickly from seed for the first two years, it gets to be two feet tall. Then its growth rate slows down considerably.

The Caribbean, where these palms grow, has been labeled one of the world's thirty-four biodiversity hot spots where we need protect the many varieties of vegetation and animal life in our custody.

Coontie *(Zamia floridana, Z. pumila, Z. integrifolia)*

Hang Out with the Coontie as the Dinosaurs Did

Before Columbus, before the Native Americans, before humans existed on the earth, coontie *(Zamia floridana)* was burying its fat tuberous root into the sandy soil and reproducing. This living fossil was a dominant form of flora during the age of dinosaurs. A relative of the cardboard and the sago palms, this cycad may be the most primitive plant on earth.

Once this plant covered much of Florida, but humans in the 1800's used its root as a food source for starch and decimated the population. One Miami mill processed ten to fifteen tons per day from 1845 to 1925. Considering that it takes thirty years to grow to a five pound tuber, the industry did not remain viable.

Making this starchy food was not an easy process as the root has cycasin, a poisonous substance, and must be macerated and washed to be edible. The Calusa and Timucua, pre-Seminole Native Americans, used it to make bread. They called it *coonti hateka* which meant white root.

Today, coontie is seldom found in the wild and it is protected from collection. It cannot be transplanted. Not that it would be easy to transplant this species, because the turnip-like tuberous root can be a yard under the soil surface and large clumps of roots could reach six feet in diameter.

However, coontie is a survivor partly because of this root. Last year, my coontie was attacked by scale and although I fought it with insecticidal soap, all of the five-inch narrow leaves died, leaving ugly three-foot dead sticks. But lo! In the spring, out of the thick stem arose new slender fronds and the entire plant recovered to its original size. Not even an asteroid hit could do in this clever, native groundcover.

This is good news for the rare *atala* butterfly *(Eumaeus atala)* because a colony of these caterpillars can consume every leaf of a female coontie. This black and blue butterfly was not declared endangered because, in 1965, experts thought it was already extinct. When landscapers began planting coontie, the butterfly reappeared and made a remarkable recovery. Coontie is an obligate host plant for the *atala* caterpillar. An obligate is an organism that needs a specific plant to survive, the way a panda needs bamboo.

The dark green plant grows very slowly to a height of three feet. That is why it is expensive ($25 for a three-gallon container) when purchased from nurseries. Its stiff fronds uncurl evenly from the stem. It grows well in full sun but just as easily could solve a deep shade problem area. Xeriscape landscapers use it because it is highly drought, wind and salt tolerant. Leaf descriptions vary slightly and this has caused a minor consternation among botanists who have various names for the *Zamia* varieties. The first description of the *Zamia pumila* came from Linnaeus in 1763. Later it was called *Z. floridana* or *Z. integrifolia*

Coontie reproduces by seed from female plants. Thin male cones grow up to ten inches long out of the stems at the end of summer. Fatter, female cones with bright red-orange seeds emerge but are not immediately receptive to fertilization. They are fertilized by a weevil *(Pharaxonotha zamiae)* which is its obligate (single) pollinator. It eats the starch-rich male cones and, attracted by odor, moves to the female cones when a change in color or temperature occurs.

These red one-inch seeds are poisonous to the human touch, but easily transported by mockingbirds and grackles, as well as rats and mice. Months later, the seed coats get soft and fall to the ground where the red outside coating is eaten off by pill bugs. My coonties are at that point now. If the seed germinates it can take five years before it is a one-foot plant. One botanist describes its growth pattern as "sleeps, creeps and leaps." It likes alkaline soil with a pH of 6 or more. (We're a pH 7-8 in Key West.)

Blue-green algae often grow near the roots. Algae have the symbiotic ability to make nitrogen from the air which encourages the growth of the coontie. There are a few pests which attack coontie: mealy bugs, scale and sooty mold. Most of them are encouraged by excessive watering. Well drained soil is a must.

Plant coontie as an evergreen ground cover under palms or pines, in the shade or sun. It is also happy potted indoors or on the porch as its leaves are wind and salt tolerant. Bonsai experts plant it in sand and artfully expose its tuberous roots. Florists often take the greens and use them in displays that they wish to last a long time. Without the coontie, a cascade of biological deaths would occur in the environment. A butterfly would no longer flap its wings and a weevil would no longer dig in the soil. What are the consequences? The dinosaurs, companions of the coontie, are extinct.

Green and Silver Thatch Palm *(Thrinax radiata, T. morrisii)*

Florida Thatch Palms Are Useful Denizens of the Keys

Years ago, along Higgs and Rest Beach, there used to be tiki huts on a broad coral beach whose thatched roofs were covered with the sturdy leaves of the *Thrinax radiata.* If a hurricane blew them off it was a simple matter to rebuild them. Replacement materials were plentiful and no one had to wait for a boat to bring them. Before that, the Seminoles used the fronds as roofing and brooms.

Their common name, thatch palms, could be because their seeds sprout prolifically, creating a "thatch of palms" growing closely together. The birds love the alluring, white seeds so much that it would be good to plant the palm in front of a window to provide a never-ending concert of bird calls. Woodpeckers, key deer, lizards, as well as various mammals, are especially fond of them.

When the foreigners (that would be us) settled here, thatch palms were used as pilings to create docks and build kraals to hold turtles before butchering them. Now the State of Florida says that the Florida thatch palm is endangered although they are widely cultivated. If no one chops one down, it will live to be 150 years old. Plant one now and it will still be here in the 22nd century. The

16

problem is that the palms grow in the strip of beach area that is exactly where the developers want to construct beach front housing. Therefore, many of them have been removed.

These palms are native to the Keys and grow *very* slowly to be anywhere from ten feet to thirty feet tall. They grow in Mexico, the Bahamas, West Indies and Central America. If the temperature gets below twenty-eight degrees they die. *Thrinax* can grow in nutrient-poor soils and glide through a hurricane. If the palm falls over, stand it back up and steady it with three stakes. As long as its roots do not stay exposed to the air, it should do fine.

Fronds emerge from the trunk spirally and the leaves are shaped in a large circle. There is a fork at the base of the frond. They are palmate (spreading like fingers from our palms) with ridges emerging from a central point. The tips of the leaves, which are separated, droop at the ends. They are planted about fifteen feet apart unless you wish to make a more natural thatch of them. When they are grown in a nursery their trunks tend to be fatter than the ones that are harvested from the wild. They love the full sun but also grow as an under-story plant.

The flowers emerge periodically throughout the year, but most frequently in the beginning of summer. Bountiful bunches of white fruit a quarter-inch across lure wildlife. The tree becomes a cornucopia of food for bees, wasps, flies and beetles. The inflorescence looks like it is alive and shimmering with activity. The flowers are bisexual or unisexual; both existing, in the same inflorescence. Although there are many kinds of wildlife to pollinate the flowers, the wind also blows pollen around. Birds play their role in propagation, happily pooping seeds all over.

Thrinax radiata's sister, *T. morrisii,* sometimes called brittle palm, is a bit smaller and more fragile. It is easy to tell them apart as *T. morrisii* is a seductive silver, while the *T. radiata* is a full green.

Botanists are having a bit of a hard time agreeing on the nomenclature of this palm. As a result, it has several names: *Thrinax floridana*, *T. multiflora*, *T. parviflora* and *T. macrocarpa*. The Spanish call the tree *palma chit*.

TREES

Black Ironwood (*Kruglodendron ferreum*)

Slim Ironwood Ideal for Xeriscaping

Two thousand one hundred years ago, Archimedes popped out of the bathtub, shouted "Eureka," (I have found it) and, in his excitement, ran naked through the streets. His bathtub discovery of specific gravity put black ironwood on the top of the heavy tree heap.

The ironwood tree is much better-behaved than the naked Archimedes, maybe because of its weightiness in the world. Put this wood in water and it straight away sinks to the bottom. Sometimes it is called leadwood for this reason. Archimedes discovery lead to the designation that one gram of water has a volume of one cubic centimeter and a specific gravity of 1.0. The lightweight balsa wood has a specific gravity of 0.17, the lignum vitae's specific gravity is 1.32, but the ironwood's is a whopping 1.42. Ironwood takes its position at the top seriously and grows very slowly, taking fifty years to reach its full height.

Our ancestors made fence posts, ax handles, cogs, rollers, cross ties and mallets from the wood. It burns slowly and evenly and was often used as firewood. I can imagine that the wood is difficult to cut with an ax since another name for the tree is musclewood. If sawed, it smells like molten lead. The Mayans made it into bows, arrows and lances. Indigenous Indians used the bark and root as a mouthwash to relieve tooth and gum ailments. In the Bahamas they used the fruit to make jams and wine. In the United States it has no commercial value.

18

The ironwood tree has a narrow trunk between four to ten inches in diameter. The bark is gray and as it ages forms long vertical ridges. Its inch and a half long leaves are an attractive, dark, glossy green. They attract cutter bees, which take circles out of the oval leaves to line their nests. The flower is small and greenish, but has copious amounts of nectar that attracts all manner of insects, butterflies and moths. It blooms year round, but more profusely in the spring and summer.

The round seeds are small and black when ripe in the fall. They are edible and are quite sweet. Birds and other animals love them and perch in the trees while they eat.

The tree grows in hardwood hammocks, often near the water, either as a shrub or a tree up to twenty-five feet in height and ten feet wide. It has a high drought tolerance once established, and takes full sun or light shade. It is a good xeriscaping tree for the Keys. It will grow from seed, but you will need to be a very patient gardener. It can withstand very high winds because it has the unusual ability to quiver in the wind.

This is a good tree as an under-story plant. Its slow growth may be an advantage as it does not need trimming. Plant it where you can lie underneath it to gaze through its lacy canopy. As a native, it has no serious diseases or insect problems.

The German botanist that named this tree was Ignatz Urban, an urbane man of the woods. He found it in Puerto Rico and called it Krug after the then German Consul. *Dendron* means tree so the moniker means Krug's tree, sure to endear Urban to the government. The second word in the name, *ferreum*, means iron-like. He classified it in the Rhamnacae family.

You can find this tree at the Key West Botanical Gardens Boardwalk Loop Tour at Stop #3. If you didn't get one at the Keys Energy giveaway, the tree is widely cultivated and available in plant nurseries for around $10.

Blolly, Beeftree (*Guapira discolor*)

Birds and Bees Hobnob in Thickets of the Blolly

Give us your poor, your tired, your winged travelers. Let them feast on the longleaf blolly or beeftree *(Guapira discolor)* as they migrate through our islands. Immigration is not difficult for these free spirits winging their way northward. Ninety miles is no great challenge when you are airborne, but you might need a rest and some chow when you arrive.

A variety of birds wing straight for the hearty, adaptable, beach-front blolly. It is a small tree with a round crown and stout trunks commonly found in coastal hammocks. Its leaves are two-inch-long with round ends that are thin when they first open and then thicken. They are light green and smooth on the top. The young branches droop from the tree when growing. Aqua-green lichens crawl all over the smooth gray trunks. When you find the lichens it's a dead give-away that you have found a blolly.

The tree shoots up quickly to twenty-five feet in height and as wide if left with multiple trunks. However it can be trained into a single trunk. It fills out after growing up. It likes moisture filled soil; however there is one growing on the beach near the Berg Bird Preserve that is growing in coral and sand that survived all the hurricanes of the last ten years. It tolerates salt spray, wind and does okay with drought. It will grow in full sun or light shade.

Male and female flowers grow on separate trees. They aren't much to look at, small and yellow-green, but the bees and butterflies seem to find them anyway. They are wind-pollinated as well as insect-pollinated and bloom year round.

The fruit of the blolly is the real prize for our wing-flapping friends. If the tree is female, bright red drupes drip from the branches. Luscious, tantalizing berries attract the fruit-eating tanagers, catbirds, and warblers. A tree full of berries is a magnificent sight. Along the coast, herons and other wading birds perch in the branches.

Lastly, the ripening crop attracts insects. The gray gnatcatcher, American redstarts and other insect-eating birds descend on the tree to eat the insects that are eating the fruit. Regrettably, invasive iguanas like them too.

Like the birds flying from other countries to our island shores the word blolly comes from across the Atlantic Ocean. In England, a loblolly is a thicket that tends to grow in moist depressions. From there comes the common name, blolly, because of the trees' propensity to grow in thick proximity to each other. The scientific name *Guapira* botanist J. F. Aublet took from indigenous words meaning to eat and bitter. *Discolor* refers to the two surfaces of the leaf being unlike in color.

A blolly is resistant to insects and diseases and have few pests. It is propagated easily from seed. It is an inexpensive purchase from local nurseries.

Blue Potato Tree *(Solanum wrightii)*

Beautiful but Dangerous Tree

When I was in Peru I went to a farmer's market where there were at least fifty different kinds of potatoes laid out in boxes on the ground. Each farmer had a different variety. There were blue ones, red ones, green ones, orange, and yellow ones. Generally, they were smaller than the potatoes we usually see and a lot more convoluted in shape. The blue potato tree, *(Solanum wrightii)* has that kind of biodiversity in its family as well. Brothers and sisters can take the shape of vines, bushes and trees. Cousins include tomatoes, eggplants, chalice vines and potatoes.

The blue potato tree made a recent entrance into the Key West Garden Club's scene as a donation from the Hopkins Nursery of Immokalee during last November's Garden Club plant sale. She's like a sexy, sinful woman...be wary about getting too close to her. She's a member of the highly poisonous nightshade family--dangerous, but amazingly beautiful. Huge, large-lobed leaves, up to a foot long, droop from her evergreen branches, but be careful. Serious spines run up the underside of the center vein on those leaves. She's not a tree you'd like to run into on a dark night in the Peruvian jungles, her country of origin, but an impressive ornament to be admired from afar.

Like her cousin, the yesterday, today and tomorrow plant, her three-inch large flowers grow in groups of three. They start a deep bluish purple, fade to lavender and end up white. The blue flowers and the potato heritage give this tree her name. She blooms all year round, opening in the morning and closing in the evening. Her long term beauty is fleeting as she will not last much more than twelve years. She needs a beautician for a regular pruning of her coiffure at least yearly. In fact, you can prune old stems right back to the base and she will cleverly shape-shift into a bush approximately seven feet tall by six feet wide.

She grows quickly and vigorously. If you give her water and full sun she'll grow to fifteen or twenty feet tall and develop a broad, fifteen-foot canopy. Mulch heavily under her canopy to keep moisture over her roots. Alkaline soil is just fine. She does well in coastal areas, but not direct salt wind.

The plant can be propagated from seed. A half-dollar size, round seed pod looks like a small green potato. When it turns brown, open it and remove the many small seeds. They should be planted in potting soil a quarter of an inch deep, and kept moist. They can also be rooted from cuttings.

This can be used as an ornamental or trimmed into a tree or a bushy barrier plant. You will find this specimen near the Butterfly Garden at the Key West Garden Club, 1100 Atlantic Boulevard. There is also one at Epcot Center in Orlando. A three gallon one is available for $12.

The blue potato tree won a Garden Merit award from the Royal Botanical Society. All your garden visitors will go "Oooooo" and "Ahhhhh."

Green Buttonwood *(Conocarpus erectus)*
Silver Buttonwood *(Conocarpus erectus var. sericeus)*

Key West Buttonwood Takes National Honors

In 1792, stock traders pledged to do business only with each other and formed the private club known as the New York Stock Exchange, under a New York buttonwood tree, thereafter known as the Buttonwood Agreement. We might be able to blame the whole financial fiasco of the market of 2008 on the convenient shade tree where they met that day in the eighteenth century, except that the stock traders' buttonwood tree was really an American sycamore.

Rather than a fiasco, we have a national honor given to the Key West green buttonwood tree on the corner of Leon and Washington St. It has been declared a National Champion Tree, as it is the largest buttonwood in the country. Stop by the corner and you will be amazed at the size of the trunk, the twists of the branches and the spread of the crown. This tree has seen many, many hurricanes. Denise Marchant, who owns the buttonwood's home, said that it had been much the same shape for the forty-six years that her family has owned the house. Locals call it the "scary tree" for obvious reasons. A sign on the tree, provided by local tree-hugger Fran Ford, establishes its pedigree. Buttonwood is a hard, dense wood and does not have growth rings, so it is not easy to determine age, but this one is probably hundreds of years old. The tree is considered native, but botanists say that it only arrived here some 5,000 years ago.

From looking at the green and silver buttonwood trees you wouldn't think that they were so closely related. The green buttonwood has shiny dark green leaves, whereas the silver buttonwood has silver-gray leaves that are covered with a mat of silky hairs. The green buttonwood trees can grow to fifty feet while the silver ones generally remain smaller, only reaching twenty-five feet.

Buttonwoods live in nutrient-poor, well-drained soil, tolerate high salt winds without injury, are drought tolerant and love the hot sun. Their elliptically shaped leaves have two excreting salt glands at the base of each leaf which increases its salt tolerance. They have tiny bursts of flowers all year long, but peak in the summer.

Picturesque and contorted when planted near the ocean winds, they can grow right behind the mangrove layer near the beaches and in coastal swamps. Planted inland, they grow more symmetrically. They exist only below the freeze line in North America because they hate the cold but also grow as far away as the Galapagos Islands and western Africa. The small, round, brown seeds float, so seed clusters can make it all the way across the oceans while retaining their vitality.

They do well as street trees and there are some nice ones planted in the median on Flagler. The versatile buttonwoods can be pruned into a four-foot hedge or allowed to grow into a handsome single-trunk, vase-shaped over fifty feet tall.

Buttonwoods can take flooding, but they don't like to sit directly in the water. You can see that in the Kitso and Berg Bird Preserves on Atlantic Boulevard, where many interior buttonwoods are dead. They grow best at about ten feet above sea level. In the Everglades, alligator nests, which are three feet above the water line, provide ideal places for their roots to take hold.

Some think that the common name comes from the round shape of the seeds that look like buttons. True, but also, buttons were actually made out of the hard wood of the tree. Their bark is high in tannin and it has been harvested commercially for that use. The wood makes high-grade charcoal and is desirable for smoking meats and fish as it burns hot and slow.

Bonsai enthusiasts love the silver trees and search for them in areas where a freeze has destroyed the mother plant. After freezes, the small bonsai plants that are prized by collectors grow out of the roots.

Buttonwoods are important hosts for air plants and are particularly good for orchids and bromeliads. Martial and amethyst hairstreak butterflies and Tantalus sphinx moths use the trees both as larval host plants and as a source of nectar. Sooty mold can attack the leaves, especially away from the coast, but it does not harm the tree.

Bravo to a buttonwood that is undaunted by the forces of nature and tenaciously lives through difficult times. This is one tough tree.

Fiddlewood (*Citharexylum fruticosum*)

Fiddle-Faddle under the Fiddlewood Tree

Last year, Keys Energy gave away fiddlewood (*Citharexylum fruticosum*) and I planted one not knowing exactly what would transpire. One year later, this multi-stemmed bush is giving me come-hither looks and showing off its glossy dark green leaves with four-inch long bracts of small, white five-petaled flowers. It perfumes the air with the smell of lilacs.

This is a plant that attracts lovers. "A loaf of bread, a jug of wine and thou, —And wilderness is Paradise now." (Omar Khayyam)

Our Paradise should have more of these romantic specimens. The State of Florida thinks so too, as it recommends the native fiddlewood (Verbenaceae family) as an outstanding ornamental that should be planted more.

When I first planted this tree I thought it would have a single trunk. However, if the many branches are not pruned off leaving only one dominant, it forms a bush that can be twenty feet high and twelve feet wide. Mine grew from two to six feet tall in one year even in our poor alkaline soil. It is drought and salt soil tolerant. It flowers prolifically in the sun in long white bracts that smell divine. It can also grow in light shade.

Round seeds form on the trees at the same time as flowers, in an orange drupe that turns brown. The fruit is edible, sweet and juicy, but two seeds take up most of the space in the fruit so there is not much pulp left. The tree can be grown from these seeds. The dense, evergreen leaves are three to six inches long with a square orange stalk and mid-rib. In the spring the leaves turn a showy orange before being shed. The trunk is brown and furrows with age.

Fiddlewood makes a great hedge and is so sturdy that it is recommended for parking lots and highways. Plant it by a window or a walkway so the floral smells can overwhelm you. It is remarkably hearty and has no major diseases or pests. Sometimes its leaves are eaten by moth caterpillars, but they have no long-term effect on the plant. It is easily pruned and, if cut to the ground, will re-grow making it hurricane resistant.

Birds love the seeds, especially hummingbirds. Bees and butterflies such as the ruddy daggerwing love the nectar. Listen up and you can hear "The buzzin' of the bees in the fiddlewood trees."

Fiddlewood comes from the West Indies and is considered invasive in Hawaii and Australia, but not here. Its name, *Citharexylum*, means lyre from the Greek word *kithara* and wood from the Greek word, *xylon*. Not surprisingly, the wood has been used in the Caribbean to make the sounding boards of string instruments, hence, *fiddle* wood. The heavy, hard wood also is used to make cabinets. An example that has been pruned to be a tree can be found at Stop # 2 of the Western Loop Tour of the Key West Botanical Gardens.

So don't fiddle-faddle. Check out a local nursery where you can get this tree for around $15. When you buy it, notice how many trunks it has to determine whether, in its soul, it wants to be a bush or a tree.

Frangipani (*Plumeria ssp.*)

Frangipani and Chanel Number 5

Frangipani and *Plumeria* are both weird words to use as a common description of an exotic plant, but in the 17th century when it was named, frangipani was as common a name as Chanel Number 5 is now. It was a perfume made from the spiral-shaped flower that the Italian 16th century Marquess Frangipani used to scent gloves, thereby hiding the leather tanning smell and fooling the customer into thinking that the gloves were as appealing as the scent.

Little did the French biologist who named it *Plumeria*, Charles Plumier, realize that the tree was also duping its main pollinator, the sphinx moth. Frangipani flowers are most fragrant at night, luring the hungry moth into the center of the flower looking for nectar, only to find it empty. They pick up pollen in their fruitless search from blossom to blossom, thereby assuring the continuation of the plant. The frangipani goes by many names in the world: temple tree, *champa*, *leelawadee*, *flor de mayo*, *himatanthus*, egg flower, *araliyia*, *lantom*, *kembang kamboja* and *cacalloxochitl* to name a few. Say them out loud. Listen to the many names of this tree to understand that this member of the Apocynaceae family grows in the wild all over the world.

Thanks to tropical storm Ike's high winds, many of the local frangipani trees lost their branches. Garden Club members propagated forty-three branches from eight different species.

The Garden Club has some of the rare red *(P. rubra)* for sale. They also have the desirable Bahama plumeria *(P. pudica)*. Its white flower has a fainter scent, but it blooms year round and retains its elongated oak-shaped, dark green leaves all winter. It is also salt wind tolerant.

Ancient Aztec and Mayan writings record the medicinal uses for the tree as an ointment. Its wood can be used for musical instruments, tableware and furniture. In the Pacific Islands it is flippantly worn in the right ear if the person is single and left ear when taken, but everyone gets to wear its flowers in leis. In India its white flowers are associated with funerals and death. Frangipani has been referenced in literature often. In Africa it has been used as a poetic symbol in the literature of love. In *The Picture of Dorian Gray,* Lord Henry's wife's frangipani perfume "lingers in the room." Shelly and Tagore also wrote about this plant, as did the less familiar authors Huysman, Couto, and the songwriter Vanderslice.

In Asia, folktales say that frangipani provides shelter for demons, vampires and ghosts. Considering how the leafless branches look in the winter, that is not surprising. Most frangipani trees take on a decidedly architectural look when all of their leaves and flowers disappear and bare branches, reminiscent of winter in the north, strike a pose against the sky. Planting them among other bushes or interesting bromeliads softens the stark shapes of the limbs. It is best to propagate at this time when they have no leaves.

The sausage-like stems of this succulent plant have a white, sticky sap which exudes from the wound when the branch is cut. It is poisonous, so don't touch it. Cast the cutting into the shade and let the sap dry up. After a week or so, plant the frangipani, stake, and wait. A three-part branch will emerge from the tip in the spring. They grow both in full sun and part shade.

Do not over water! In fact, do not water at all in the winter. All kinds of diseases attack this non-native plant, and if you over water you are likely to attract one of them. Rust fungus, black tip fungus, mealy bugs, scale, spider mites, whiteflies, stem rot, snails, slugs, grasshoppers, and sun scald are a few. These usually do not attack trees that are not over-watered.

Frangipani can grow to twenty-six feet with multiple trunks as large as thirteen feet in circumference. They grow very quickly and can easily shoot up to twelve feet in as little as six years. This is a wonderful pot plant because it can be easily pruned into whatever shape the gardener chooses. It can be grown as a bonsai. Look for a plant that has a short trunk before it branches out and it can become a hedge or a screen.

Geiger Tree (*Cordia sebestena*)

Flashy Orange Blossoms Grace the Geiger Tree

In the spring, birders stop to gape at the flamboyant Geiger tree (*Cordia sebestena*) that still stands in front of the Audubon House on Whitehead Street as they remember the white-crowned pigeons Audubon painted in its branches in 1832. If they are lucky, they get to see the threatened pigeons which Bill Merritt, Operations Manager at the Audubon House, says still visit each spring.

Audubon described the original tree as "fifteen feet high with a trunk of five inches." The tree is now thirty feet tall and has a trunk with a circumference of 51 inches. If it is the same tree, It could be well over 200 years old. How's that for hurricane survival? Although named after the Key West wrecker Captain John H. Geiger whose yard contained the tree, according to recent archeological findings, the Geiger tree existed in Florida long before the Europeans came. Roger L. Hammer says seeds *might* have floated here as they are buoyant, but he believes that Geiger planted this particular one.

The Geiger has great smelling, three-inch, white fruit, but Merritt says the pigeons prefer figs and poison wood fruit. The Geiger fruit is not very tasty, but people who have eaten the kernels say they taste like filberts. The seeds can be propagated and sometimes sprout underneath the mother tree.

The Geiger tree is a favorite because of its huge orange blossoms which flower near evergreen leaves as large as a man's hand. If there is a drought, the tree will drop its leaves to conserve energy and survive. Caribbean people used the rough-textured leaves as sandpaper to smooth tortoise shells. The tree blooms profusely all year when young and less frequently when older. It doesn't care a whit what the soil is like and wades right through saltwater floods. In full sun it grows at a moderate rate to reach thirty feet in height by twenty-five feet in width.

A group of botanists from Connecticut College watched a Geiger tree for 5.3 hours and recorded 191 visits of hummingbirds to the bright orange flowers. (There *are* people like that.) The nectar also attracts butterflies and bees.

If you are sick, this is your tree, as it is reputed to have medicinal effects for catarrh, edema, malaria, incontinence and venereal diseases. The tree comes from the Borage family. The name *Cordia* comes from Valerius Cordus, a 16th Century German botanist. *Sebestena* refers to a Persian tree with similar seeds found near the town of Sebesta. Egyptian mummy cases were made out of the wood.

Plant this tree as a specimen in a prominent place in the yard or amongst other vegetation. It can be a street tree or a median strip tree or a parking lot tree.

The tree sometimes looks trashy with leaves destroyed by the flashy, green Geiger beetle but the leaves grow right back. It can be a bit of a litterbug, but it is sure showy when grown in the midst of other vegetation. It has no diseases of any note. The City of Key West has recently planted these trees on Rest Beach and down the median on Flagler Avenue.

Gumbo Limbo *(Bursera simaruba)*

Gumbo Limbo Trees Have the Last Laugh against Winds

During the Sculpture Key West installation in the Key West Garden Club after Hurricane Wilma, I noticed a stone marker indicating that there was a piece of artwork in the Butterfly Garden, but I did not see anything that I recognized as sculpture. It was only when I stood in the back of the garden that I suddenly saw what had been created by the artist. Perched in the bare branches of a gumbo limbo *(Bersera simaruba)* were a plethora of small black-feathered birds.

The deciduous gumbo limbo normally loses its leaves around March. This one did not have leaves for almost a year after Hurricane Wilma according to Rosi Ware, president of the Key West Garden Club. Gumbo limbos can lose their leaves in a drought as well as a hurricane but are undamaged, as they can make chlorophyll utilizing their bark. This one was a survivor and is still gracing the butterfly garden.

This is the kind of native tree that we should clone, and it is easy enough to do, although some say that cloned trees are not as strong as trees grown from seeds unless they are pruned carefully. Cut a branch off of the tree, stick it in the ground and watch as a new tree emerges. In fact, you could take a twelve-inch trunk, bury it in the ground, and it will grow. People have used the trunks, placed closely together, to grow a fence quickly.

This common canopy tree is frequently found planted along the streets and can grow to sixty feet in height. Its large, open form makes it a great shade tree as wide as it is tall. If its

32

feathery compound leaves are smashed, they smell like turpentine and make a tea used for dysentery. I don't recommend a tea that tastes like turpentine.

The tree is easily recognized by its trunks' oily, red skin that peels off to expose green bark. Key West locals call it the "tourist tree" because like the tourists, it is often red and peeling. If it is scoured by hurricanes, the trunk can be covered with a sensual, silvery gray patina. The gummy resin has been used to make glue, varnish and liniment. The Calusa Indians used the tree's sticky bark resin to trap birds. The trees in its torchwood family (*Burseraceae)* are used for incense, and include the trees that produce frankincense, (*Boswellia carterii*) and myrrh, *(Commiphora erythraea)*.

The soft, spongy wood is easily carved and was used to make carousel horses before they were molded out of plastic. It has been used for matches, toothpicks, charcoal, crates, boxes and interior trim. In case you are compelled to make a canoe out of a tree trunk, its resin is handy for coating the outside of the canoe to keep it watertight. Haitians prize gumbo limbo for its wood from which they make drums.

The tree has inconspicuous, cream colored flowers, both male and female blooming at the same time. One or two hard, red seeds appear in a three-part capsule throughout the year. The two-inch leaves are shiny, bright green on the top and lighter on the bottom and arranged alternately on the stems. They are compound and have tapered tips. As with most natives, gumbo limbos are drought and salt tolerant and can take the high winds of a hurricane without a problem. Salt wind turns the leaves brown but the tree bounds back quickly. It grows best in the sun in alkaline, sandy, well drained, nutrient-deficient soil.

Wildlife love the tree, as its leaves provide larval food and its flowers provide nectar for the dingy purplewing butterfly *(Eunica monima).* It is believed that mockingbirds, flycatchers and vireos eat the attractive but mostly inedible one-fourth inch triangular seeds for the same reason that chickens eat pebbles, to grind up food in their crops.

Gumbo limbo trees with bougainvillea growing up their limbs make a lovely combination. *Monstera* also looks good climbing into the thick branches. A National Champion gumbo limbo is at St. Mary's Star of the Sea Church on Truman Avenue. Sprouting seeds from this tree in order to produce sturdy offspring would be a good community project.

Tree of Life (*Lignum vitae* or *Guaiacum sanctum)*

Garden Club Gives Tree of Life New Life

In myth, the wood of the lignum vitae tree was found in the Garden of Eden and was used for the Holy Grail; therefore it was called holy wood. Whoever consumed its resin was to be given perpetual health, immortality, and protected from weakness and infirmity. Merlin's staff was made of the wood, as was the bathtub in Gabriel Garcia Marquez's book *Love in the Time of Cholera.*

The Native Americans taught the Spanish how to extract its resin to make purges, cathartics and antiseptics, treating arthritis, rheumatism, syphilis and tuberculosis. It was the penicillin of its day. It is still used in modern medicine in certain blood tests. It was originally brought to Europe by Christopher Columbus who declared that "it was immune to all destructive organisms." By 1500 its wood was regularly shipped from the Florida Keys to Europe. Later, timber cutters from the Bahamas decimated large tracts of *Lignum vitae* forests. It could neutralize poisons and served as a contraceptive. It was made into dishes, mallets, bowling balls, butcher blocks, guitar picks and Billy clubs.

Many of the trees were destroyed from 1850 to 1900 when the land in the Florida Keys was cleared for agricultural plantations. One cubic foot weighs 82 pounds and the tree, whose specific gravity is 1.39, sinks when immersed in water. The Garden Club has a very heavy *Lignum vitae* stump a foot high in the orchid room.

Because of its hardness it was desired by shipbuilders. The Navy used it in WW II to make the submarine propeller shaft bearings for the USS Pampanito. The hinges and locks made from the wood lasted over 100 years in the Erie Canal. It was called *el palo para muchas cosas*, the wood of many uses, and that was its downfall. The wood may have been long lasting, but the stock of living trees never recovered.

The public interest raised in an article in a 1968 *Natural History Magazine* resulted in Lignum vitae Key Botanical State Park (MM 78.5) being declared a protected historic site. However the tree is still endangered and exists in the U.S. only in the Florida Keys.

The tree has three or four pairs of bright green leaflets about one inch long. Because its wood is thirty percent resin it is self-lubricating. Once sanded, the surface of the wood looks like it has been varnished. Clusters of rare, bright blue flowers with five petals attract bees and butterflies, especially the obligate *Kricogonia lysid* (*sulpher lysid*), for which the tree is its only larval food. Red seeds cover a black core and exist in an orange, five-part seed pod that pops open throughout the year.

The native tree grows to a height of twenty-five feet and can be a foot and a half in diameter. Its bark is pale gray and rough. Because its growth rings are not distinct, it is difficult to determine a tree's age. A full grown example is just to the left at the entrance to the gardens of the Garden Club and there is one in the Key West Cemetery. There are six species in the Zygopyllaceae family and the larger-leafed Cuban version is planted in the native section of the garden on the hill. In the cemetery in the Otto family's fenced section, the one with the little deer in it, is an old *Lignum vitae* that has a trunk over four feet in circumference. The National Champion tree is found on St. Mary''s Star of the Sea grounds.

It is difficult to propagate, but the Key West Garden Club has taken a special interest in growing this endangered tree. The *Lignum Vitae* "Wood of Life" Conservation Project endeavors to introduce more of these trees into the Keys. Many sizes of specimens are available for sale at the Garden Club. Since they are slow growing, the larger trees sell first at the Garden Club sales events. They bonsai very well.

Paradise Tree *(Simarouba glauca)*

Native Paradise Tree More Useful Than Google

The paradise tree is a marvelous creation. It mops up carbon dioxide and produces oxygen. Its leaves provide shade and then fall to the ground as life-giving mulch. Its deep roots prevent soil erosion. One acre of trees can eat 500 kg of carbon dioxide in a year. It grows in wastelands where other farm products won't grow, doesn't need water, is easily propagated from seeds or cuttings and it is a cash crop. It is believed it is named "paradise tree" because it can live only in a frost-free environment, such as our "Paradise," the Florida Keys.

This tree's seed produces edible oil which is used in baking in Central America and India. It is often called oil tree or bitterwood. The oil does not contain bad cholesterol. The oilseed cake (what's left after the oil is squeezed out) is full of nitrogen, phosphorus and potash and makes a good fertilizer. Its shells can be used to make particle board and the termite-resistant wood can be used to make furniture, toys, matches and paper. The fruit pulp is sweet and is used to make beverages when the birds don't eat them.

Every part of the tree is used for medicinal purposes. Natives use it to cure intestinal parasites, fevers, malaria, diarrhea, dysentery, anemia, colitis, herpes, influenza, polio, West Nile virus and other viruses, stomach and bowel disorders, as an astringent for wounds and sores, to stop bleeding and as a tonic. It is currently being studied as a toxin to cancer and leukemia cells. Quite a list! It is purported to cure everything from a tummy ache to cancer. If that is not enough, it is also used as a skin toner. It improves hydration, helping to retain moisture and will get rid of liver spots. This tree is more useful than Google.

The miracle substances found in the paradise tree are quassinoids. Several of the four-syllable substances found in the quassinoids, have been known to scientists for years. Currently, a number of experiments are being done with them.

In parts of the world where the sustainability of farming is in question because of global warming that has created droughts, this member of the Simaroubaceae family can be planted and six years later, the first crop of fruit can be harvested. The wasteland can sustain a large population and the tree will gradually improve the soil. It can live to be a seventy-year-old granddad. Termites don't attack it, cattle, goats and sheep do not eat it, and it has virtually no pests. It's a safe bet that deer also do not like it. Economically viable and ecologically sustainable, this is a tree for the twenty-first century.

The paradise tree is native to Key West and, like all natives, is salt water, drought and salt wind tolerant, (although it loses branches easily). Alkaline soil is its caviar. Towering above the tropical Florida hammocks forty feet high is its large round crown enjoying full sun. Thick, rough, dark gray bark covers its trunk and branches. Its tiny yellow flowers occur on female and male trees. The females are bigger producers of seeds than males and so agronomists are trying to graft the most productive trees to increase the output of the oil. The bright red drupes turn black when they get ripe and can be a bit of a litter problem if they are planted by the roadsides. Birds love them but they will stain sidewalks. A second problem with this tree is that its roots remain near the surface and can push up sidewalks and roads.

Pinnate leaves (a single stem from which leaves branch off) with alternate, oblong leaf arrangement, (which is pretty sophisticated as trees go), emerge a creamy, copper-red, like dusting the tree with paprika before they turn green. If you plant one now it is so fast growing that it will be big before your kids are. Propagation is from seed which germinates quickly and grows rapidly. You can see this tree at the Key West Garden Club in the native garden.

The western world is busy discovering the many uses of the aptly named paradise tree.

Royal Poinciana (*Delonix regia*)

Flamboyant Royal Poinciana Is Conspicuous in the Keys

Ever wonder why the poinciana tree and the poinsettia Christmas plant sound similar? Phillipe de Lonviliers de Poincy, the first French governor of St. Kitts, built himself a fortified mansion called La Fontaine with an exotic botanical garden. Both of these plants, imported from Madagascar, were named after him. When his French replacement arrived, Poincy declared his island a sovereign state and sent the replacement packing back to France, in chains. St. Kitts seceded from France and Key West seceded from the U.S. making them similar island nations. La Fontaine was started in 1642. Surely this must have been one of the first botanical gardens in the Caribbean.

The scientific name, *Delonix* comes from the Greek *delos* meaning conspicuous and *onux* meaning claw for the flower's four clawed petals. *Regia* means royal and it certainly is the queen of trees having been voted into the top five most beautiful flowering trees in the world, although I don't believe I ever saw a French queen dressed in its flamboyant orange red.

On a musical note, the seed pods are used as an Antillian *shak-shak* or maraca. Native American story tellers use the seed pods to call spirit friends. In Barbados, slaves used this instrument, banjos and bones to create music that was forbidden by the British government.

This is a messy tree. High winds rip branches off, scattering them all over. The flowers drop after blooming in June and July and make a mess under the tree. The eighteen-inch long seed pods are noisy and create an obstacle course when they fall to the ground. Send the kids out to collect them if you have a fireplace, as in the Caribbean the seed pods are used for fuel. High maintenance, yes, but its incredible beauty during the eight spring weeks it blooms every year makes it all worthwhile. Even when not blooming, the tree has an Asian grace. Feathery compound leaves are only two inches long, but are on branches that are thirty inches long, and then spread into secondary branches that have twenty to forty pairs of pinnate leaves, followed by the last branch which has ten to twenty pairs of pinule leaves. The branches float like feathers in the breeze.

The tree quickly grows to forty feet in height and spreads its crown to sixty feet in width, with a great red umbrella of flowers. Choosing the right spot to plant it is important. Keep it ten feet away from driveways and sidewalks as its roots will undermine them. It provides great shade, but it is difficult to grow grass underneath. It reseeds itself readily.

Using an arborist to prune while your tree is young is important to develop strong branches that won't be damaged in high winds. Interestingly, royal poinciana can be used to bonsai and as a container plant, even grown inside. It is identified as both in the Leguminosae (bean) family and the Fabaceae (pea) family.

The tree grows at a rate of five feet per year and doesn't flower until it is at least five years old. It is best to buy one that is already flowering. A three-gallon plant sells for $40. If you are a patient gardener you can plant the seed after scarifying it (nicking it to remove the first layer). There is also a yellow variety called *D. flavida* that you can see at the Garden Club.

Poinciana is drought and salt tolerant and prefers dry winters, full sun, and alkaline, well-drained soil. After it is established it is an excellent xeriscaping plant. The State of Florida says that it has "excellent ornamental features and could be planted more."

It does not attract any particular wildlife except occasional ambrosia beetles. It could pick up ganoderma root rot if the soil is too moist, not likely here in the Keys.

Miami has a Poinciana Festival each spring. Certainly Key West has enough of these glamorous queens to start its own horticultural festival.

Seagrape *(Coccoloba uvifera)*

Crazy Coccoloba Is a Tropical Treasure

I discovered several of the many uses of the native, dried seagrape leaf with Girl Scout Troop 101 from Sugarloaf Key. Last Christmas, their leader, Debra Jo Clem, gave them a project to sew the leaves together to make wreaths and to draw or write messages on their dry smooth surfaces with colored markers. Page Clem drew a coral reef on her leaf. Pull out your acrylics and paint invitations to a beach party on the dry surfaces of the leaves or if you are less creative, try writing your grocery list on one. Before drying and turning brown, their red colors make a striking addition to a flower arrangement.

Protected from winds in the interior, the seagrape *(Coccoloba uvifera)* could reach sixty feet in height. In the Keys, however, it is usually found along coastal areas and, since high winds associated with storms snap its brittle branches, the tree often remains low and is as wide as it is high. Chances are that this cutie will look more like a ten foot bush with round bangles clanking around her limbs than a tree.

Round leaves that can grow up to twelve inches across make this specimen one of the most unusual trees inhabiting the Keys. Leaves emerge from a bud protected from salt winds by mucilage. They're a soft and sensuous bronzed-pink when they emerge. Then they harden to a bright green with red veins and stems and finally transform into a brilliant russet-red. Floating like Frisbees to the ground, they slowly dry, coating the ground with a pale brown rug.

Thin, splotchy bark covers the seagrape's massive, two-foot-in-diameter trunks that support stout branches. Branches can be cut off, planted and will grow into new trees. Kids love climbing the sturdy limbs.

In the summer, the seagrape blooms with small, white flowers on long racemes. These

40

turn into deep purple grapes in the late summer. Not every tree will have fruit as there are male and female trees. Seagrapes can be propagated from seeds, but just because you planted a seed from a female tree does not mean that you will get a female tree. *Coccoloba* is in the Polygonaceae (buckwheat) family.

A bunch of grapes ripens unevenly so in order to harvest them (if you can get there before the birds eat them), place a large sheet under the tree and shake the tree. The ripe grapes will fall to the ground and to be scooped up in the sheet. Jellies, jams and wine can be made from the fruit.

Seagrape Jelly

1 quart sea grape juice
5 tablespoons lemon or lime juice
1 package powdered pectin
5 cups sugar

To prepare juice: Wash sea grapes and measure out two cups. Put in fairly large, wide pot with half as much water (1 cup water to 2 cups sea grapes.) Bring to a boil. Mash often with a potato masher and continue boiling until fruit is reduced to a soft pulp (about 25 to 30 minutes). Drain through a jelly bag or several layers of cheesecloth. Do not squeeze.

Place one quart juice in a wide kettle. Turn heat high and add lemon or lime juice and pectin. Bring mixture to a rolling boil. Stir in sugar and return to a rolling boil. Boil hard for 1 minute, stirring constantly. Remove from heat. Skim foam if necessary. Pour into hot, sterilized jars, leaving 1/4-inch head space. Adjust caps. Process 5 minutes in boiling water bath (If you use unripe seagrapes as well as ripe ones you can eliminate the pectin).

Many species are fond of the seagrape. It provides significant food and cover for wildlife and is courted by the Florida dusky wing butterfly, Julia and Schaus' swallowtail.

The seagrape will withstand salt water inundation, drought and salt winds. It grows in sandy, well-drained soil and thrives in full sun. A freeze will damage the tree so it is not found north of sub-tropical zones. If you cut a sea grape branch and put the end in the ground it will grow into a new plant.

Medicinally, a gum from the bark is used for throat ailments and the roots for treating dysentery. The wood is prized for cabinets and, if it is boiled, makes a red dye. In landscaping, seagrapes can be pruned to be a hedge or a fence. There is a hedge row of them across from Smather's Beach.

Seven-year apple *(Casasia clusiifolia)*

Hardy Seven Year Apple Is a Denizen of the Beach

Ironically, the seven year apple is neither an apple nor does it take seven years for its fruit to mature. It is in the Rubiaceae family. This leathery denizen of beach fronts manages to flower and form fruit at the same time, which is a good thing because it takes a full year for the fruit to ripen. When it does ripen it is devoured by mockingbirds that hollow out the tasty fruit and leave a dead skin hanging in the tree. Butterflies such as the Tantalus sphinx *(Aeliopus tantalus),* use it as a larval host plant, and the mangrove skipper *(Phocides pigmalion)* and others that use it for nectar, float around it.

This small tree or shrub grows well along the coastline. Although it can't take sitting in salt water like the mangrove, it does well directly on the coastline where it gets inundated with storm water. It can withstand hurricane force winds and come back with new leaves. This is one tough plant.

The seven-year apple has six-inch, shiny, leaves that curl inward. They are thick, long, oval, and are clustered near the branch tips. It has five-petalled clusters of white flowers with pink edges that emerge mostly in the spring and early summer, but can be found all year long. Male and female flowers are on different plants. The flowers have a magnificent smell and could easily be used in perfume. *Eau de Casasia* could be a big seller if the perfumers ever find enough of it.

Fruits emerge as small, hard, green orbs shaped like pears. They hang on the tree while they turn yellow, dark brown and then black. When they are dark brown they are sweet and ready to eat, but beware of the many seeds. They are probably best left to the mockingbirds. These seeds are prolific and can be propagated easily.

The native seven-year apple is only found in the southern-most tip of Florida, the Florida Keys and in the Caribbean. A slow grower, often it is as wide as it is tall, reaching a top height of fifteen feet. It has a dense round crown. The seven-year apple grows in part shade and sun, but I have only seen them thriving in full sun. Their soil must be porous; sand and rocks are ideal. Our alkaline limestone will do just fine. They survive in the second tier away from a beach. Their drought and salt wind tolerance are high. Because it is native, there are no serious pests found on the plant.

Planted close together, they grow into a full hedge or screen. They are great as wind breaks near the ocean. Although the fruits are fairly ugly, the flowers are showy and, my, that smell! They make lovely specimen shrubs. They can withstand median strip planting or survive in a parking lot island. Try growing them in large pots on the patio or balcony as they can take the strong ocean winds and not get wind burn. If you want to see one, take a look out at Ft. Zachary Taylor beside the road as you come into the park.

Although its name may be mysterious, it holds a strong niche in the Keys environment.

Shaving Brush Tree *(Bombax ellipticum)*

Comical Bombax Flowers Provide Neighborhood Drama

Drama occurs daily on the streets of Key West, but on Eaton Street, every night in the spring a leafless tree provides the neighborhood with a show unlike any other. Six-inch flower buds grow in terminal clusters on the branches on the bizarre *Bombax ellipticum*. At sunset, velvety-brown petals begin to roll back in five sections and the innumerable rose-pink flowers that look like old fashioned shaving brushes, burst open with an audible pop. Each flower is tipped with yellow pollen like the soap on the end of the brush.

Within fifteen minutes, the tree is covered with blossoms. During the night, insects pollinate the flowers. Over the course of the next day, the blossoms fall off the tree. They will keep several days even without water. The calyxes stay on the tree. These develop into capsules as long as six inches where the seeds encased in cotton grow. This cotton can be spun into thread, but it has short strands and therefore is not easy to work. It is used for stuffing mattresses and sleeping bags. Often it is used in life jackets because it has five times the buoyancy of cork.

This show-stopping drama occurs nightly for about six weeks. If that isn't enough excitement, each day, depending on your disposition, the tree leaves either a horrible mess or a beautiful polka dot pattern on the lawn.

After flowering, maroon leaves emerge and then turn green. The tree is deciduous and drops its leaves in the fall, which makes it look fairly homely all winter. Smooth, gray and green streaked bark covers a swollen trunk. Because it is leafless much of the year, the green bark takes over the process of photosynthesis to make chlorophyll. The wood of this tree is unusual, having stripes of greens, browns, yellows, and whites. Its showy nature also makes it a favorite for bonsai enthusiasts.

The outline of the tree is massive, forty feet tall and equally as wide and it is buttressed with huge roots. Its thick limbs spread like an octopus making this an excellent climbing tree for kids.

The tree is native to the Yucatan in Mexico and is drought tolerant, but not highly salt tolerant and thrives in full sun. It is an excellent xeriscaping plant. The Mayans call it chac kuyche. It is often called kapok, which refers to the silky fibers found in the seed pods, but that is inaccurate. The single tree that is a true kapok is *Ceiba pentandra* and is not common in Florida. However, there is a magnificent specimen in front of the Key West court house on Whitehead Street (the one with the "End of the Rainbow" sign near it).

In this family, there is also a tree called *Pseudobombax ellipticum* which has white flowers. Many trees in the Bombacaeae family have trunks covered with blunt thorns when they are young.

Native American Nahau women in Veracruz, Mexico have traditionally used parts of the tree to treat toothache, coughs, fever and ulcers. They believe it will establish a hot/cold equilibrium.

This messy jack-in-the-box may not be for your front yard, but take a stroll down Eaton Street at dusk in the spring and watch the flashy flowers pop out.

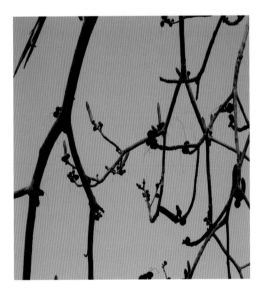

Smooth Strongback (*Bourreria succulenta*)

Endangered Smooth Strongback Perfumes the Air

Roger Hammer, the renowned botanist, was speaking with a Bahamian restaurateur about bush medicine when the confusion between the names smooth strongback and Bahama strongbark came up. She told him that women make a tea from the leaves to give their husbands a "strong back." When he asked if that was for lifting things she replied with great laughter, "Oh, no, no, no, mon!"

The *Bourreria succelenta* (or *B. ovata*) is also known as bodywood or pigeon berry. It is fairly common in the Florida Keys' hammocks. The rest of Florida should be jealous as it is rare in other places. It has aromatic, half-inch, white blossoms fill the breezes with perfume all year, but peak in the summer and fall. You'll recognize it by its bright red drupe of berries and those fragrant little white flowers. It is listed as endangered by the State of Florida.

This is a large shrub or small tree with vine-like droopy branches that cascade toward the ground. Its three-inch, shiny green leaves start out rough and later become smooth. It grows at a moderate rate and normally doesn't get to be more than twenty feet tall, a fifteen feet wide crown and six inches in circumference. Joseph Nemac, a park ranger at Key Largo Hammock Botanical

State Park, is credited with finding a rare rough strongback at Crocodile Lake National Wildlife Refuge that holds the record for "American Forests' Big Trees." It is 32 inches in circumference, 28 feet tall and 14 feet wide. Using the Big Tree rating system it scores a measly 64. By way of comparison, Key West holds the record for the largest mahogany with a 278-point champion. Speaking of records, the Florida Keys have more species of native trees (110) than any comparable area in North America.

Certain trees have excellent genetic qualities and grow to be very old, just as there are some humans who grow to be very old. St. Mary's Star of the Sea children are currently propagating seeds from just such a "Champion" tree found on their church grounds. They might be willing to give up a few of their seeds for home propagation if you didn't get a tree when Keys Energy gave them away. The seed takes a couple of months to sprout. The smooth strongback can be propagated from de-pulped and scarified seeds.

The smooth strongback has some cousins around Key West. Some rough strongback (*B. radula*) specimens are growing at the Key West Cemetery near the "I told you I was sick," gravestone. A third rare member of this family found in the Keys, the little pineland strongback (*B. cassinifolia*) was sold at the Botanical Gardens plant sale last year. All are listed as rare and endangered.

This tree is a native so, as usual, it loves the nutrient poor soil, can take long droughts and salty winds. It likes full sun but does well with light shade, too. Because it is native, it has few pests or diseases.

The birds, especially the migrating ruby-throated hummingbirds, mockingbirds and catbirds adore the tree and use it both for cover and for food. Bahamian swallowtails, giant swallowtails, Julies, large orange sulphurs, mangrove skippers, southern broken-dashes and other butterflies enjoy its nectar.

The Irish naturalist, Patrick Browne (1720-1790), immigrated to Jamaica and named the genus after his friend, a German apothecary, Johann Ambrosius Beurer (1716-1754.) It was subsequently misspelled and turned into *Bourreria*. If a branch is cut it bleeds milky white sap inspiring the name *succulenta*.

Plant this tree where you can get a whiff of its flowers and watch the birds and butterflies it attracts.

Spanish Stopper (*Eugenia foetida*)

Confab with Frothy Fairies on the Spanish Stopper

The white flowers of the Spanish stopper (*Eugenia foetida*) cluster around the branches of the tree creating froth that looks like a tiny fairy confab. Every fairy breath flings fragrance into the air with abandon. When the wind catches the branches, the fairies dance a Spanish fandango.

Like the magical people of the Keys, the Spanish stopper can juggle several jobs at the same time, flowering and fruiting all year. The small, edible berries turn orange and then black and provide food for a variety of birds. Key deer do not like to eat the leaves, maybe because of their smell.

The leathery, dark green leaves have a musky smell that accounts for the scientific name *foetida* which means malodorous or stinking. There are no veins seen in the leaf. The oval, inch-long leaf smells a little like skunk when crushed, but the flowers more than make up for the odor. *Eugenia* means flowering for this plant which is in the Myrtaceae family.

Unlike many Keys trees, the stopper has a deep tap root and lateral root system, allowing it to grow in the most difficult of places, such as a crack in a rock. Give the tree some rubble, clay or rocky soil and it thrives. Drought tolerant, salt wind tolerant and able to take a short flood makes the stopper a highly desirable tree.

The plant is used as an accent shrub or small tree and is a pioneering plant (the first to emerge) in costal hammocks and thickets. Accustomed to growing under taller trees, it doesn't need full sun. Several slim, erect trunks grow to create a rounded crown. Sometimes the tree is pruned to have a single trunk and grows to a narrow twenty-five feet tall. The trunk gets concentric circles on the bark when older. Orange underbark shows up when the older bark peals away. It can be trimmed so that the beautiful bark on the many trunks can be displayed.

The name stopper refers to its medicinal use. The reddish bark can be used to make a tea that is used to treat diarrhea. When it works, you can see where the name "stopper" originates. In modern times it might be called "Montezuma's miracle" tree. Because it is a native, there are no serious pests or diseases that affect it.

Many butterflies love the stopper's nectar filled flowers, especially the long-lived, Zebra longwing, Florida's state butterfly.

Because of their many small branches, stoppers can be used as hedges or screens, street trees, or even as specimen trees. The growth rate is moderate to slow. The largest one on the Champion Tree record has a circumference of sixteen inches. Propagated from seeds, it takes a couple of months before germinating. For indoor gardeners, it is a good candidate for bonsai. The State of Florida says that the plant "has outstanding ornamental features and could be planted more."

Years ago, according to Kevin M. McCarthy in *Christmas in Florida,* "Most people placed a Spanish stopper tree in their houses decorated with seashells, handmade decorations and even light bulbs found along the shore. To paint the tree they mixed the juices of prickly-pear, berries and bluing. They secured candles to the branches with two pronged clothes pins."

There are other stoppers, Simpson's, red, redberry, and white. While they are similar, each has its own particular eye-catching beauty.

Three-gallon red or Simpson's stoppers can be purchased at MARC House for $10 and seven-gallon ones for $60-$95. Mama's Garden Center's seven-gallon Spanish stoppers fare $40.

If you'd like a brief encounter with one of the white poofy fairies that reside on this tree, try Stop #9 at the Key West Botanical Gardens.

Spicewood Tree (*Calyptranthes pallens*)

Inhale Exotic Spices When Clipping a Spicewood Hedge

You don't have to go to the jungles of Brazil to find new anti-cancer drugs. Forget the rainforest; Key West has its own native pharmacy of medicines in the spicewood tree (*Calyptranthes pallens*). The University of Illinois at Chicago has researched the anti-cancer effects of a chemical that they found in its leaves and twigs and found it active against human oral carcinoma.

The Cherokee made a tea sweetened with honey from its branches that they called AH-DEE-TAH-STEE. They used it to treat upset stomachs and sleeplessness. Revolutionary War soldiers drank it when they ran out of coffee (They might have had a few upset tummies and a bit of sleeplessness, too).

This multi-trunked, tree/shrub grows at a moderate rate to twenty by ten feet as undergrowth in hardwood hammocks. Beautiful pale burgundy baby leaves emerge before they slowly turn a dark green. When young they are covered with rusty hairs to discourage predators from eating them. Full grown, the leaves are three inches long--dense, compact and evergreen.

When they are crushed they smell exotically spicy. Who needs showy flowers when there are leaves like this? Take pride in planting this tree that is listed as threatened by the State of Florida.

Spicewood can be trained to be either a tree or a shrub. It thrives in partial shade or full sun and can take damp soil, but once established, is drought and salt soil tolerant. Nutrient-poor soils nurture this tree like broccoli nurtures us. Salt wind may burn its leaves, so don't plant it right on the ocean. Spicewood has no major pests or diseases and is definitely a xeriscaping star.

Its tiny white flowers are inconspicuous from spring to fall, but their fragrance forms a cloud that hovers around the branches. The flowers are bisexual and polygamous. Young, smooth bark becomes scaly as it ages, just like us.

Many species of birds delight on the small round fruit of this desirable plant in the Myrtaceae family as it turns from green to yellow to red to black. It will attract the varied voices of mockingbirds, cardinals and woodpeckers. Small birds take cover in the thick foliage and bees and butterflies are attracted to the flowers.

This plant may be used as a specimen or planted as a superior hedge. Pruning it is a pleasure as it perfumes the air with spice when its leaves are cut. As a small tree, it can be used in parking lots or median strips in highways. That means it's tough. It will survive hurricanes. It would be good sun cover for a window air conditioner. It's available through nurseries that specialize in native Florida plants. A three-gallon size is $7.50. Do not mistake it for Spice bush, (*Lendera benzoin*) a totally different plant.

Wild Lime, Prickly-ash *(Zanthoxylum fagara)*

Wild Lime Cat-claw Hooks Wait for Human Invaders

Pity the poor surveyors of Flagler's railroad when they were struggling through the native Keys vegetation and they came upon a thicket of wild limes. The mosquitoes might have been horrendous, but another formidable adversary lay in wait, tempting the men with their lushly-lime perfumed leaves. The thorns on the wild lime, *(Zanthoxylum fagara)* could rip them apart, creating nasty skin tears subject to infection.

This multi-trunk, tree/bush can grow to twenty feet in height and width. It has small irregularly shaped branches imbedded with sharp, hooked spines. In Spanish, wild lime is called *una de gatos,* referring to a female cat's sharp claws. Small, compound, bright green leaves adorn the branches of this native plant.

Sadly, it bears no limes, but it does attract the caterpillar of the giant swallowtail butterfly *(Papilio cresphontes)* that much prefers its leaves to its secondary choice, your key lime tree. The caterpillars look like bird droppings, but a six and a half inch wingspan gives the yellow and black butterfly A+ garden credentials. The wild lime also attracts the rare Schaus' swallowtail butterfly. Deer like to nibble wild lime leaves.

Just as a wild lime thicket is impenetrable to humans, it is also impenetrable to predatory animals, resulting in excellent nesting sites for small birds. The nectar from the small yellow flower attracts insects. Birds like both insects and seeds, so it attracts both fruit eating and insect eating birds.

Makasuki Seminoles made bows and arrows from the wood. They used the plant to treat stomach ache, poor circulation, syphilis and as a stimulant and diuretic.

Zanthoxylum, the scientific name, means yellow in Greek. The wood produces a yellow dye and the tiny stem-mounted flowers are also yellow and bloom all year. The black fruit is contained in orange-brown follicles. The word *fagara* refers to its peppery qualities. Some species of prickly-ash seeds are used as a spicy condiment, especially in Chinese cooking. Lime leaves are called for in some curry recipes. They are not eaten, but removed before serving, like bay leaves.

You can plant this right next to the water as salty wind doesn't bother it. Once it is established, it can thrive in nutrient poor soils with a high pH and little water. It likes full sun, but can tolerate shade. This is our kind of xeriscaping plant. Wild Lime has no serious pests, but there have been rumors that it is a host plant for citrus greening disease.

There aren't many of these around Key West that are grown-ups, but since Keys Energy gave them away this spring, we are bound to have some big ones in a few years. You can see small ones growing between the rocks at the beach end of Bertha Street. We'll see how they survive the salt water intrusion at that vulnerable spot. For $7.50 you can get a specimen that is about three feet tall.

The wild lime is used as a buffer strip between homes or on highway medians. It can even take the salt wind as a container plant on ocean-facing balconies. This lacy, terrorist plant combined with some yucca will keep everything but nesting birds at bay, so if you have a fence that you don't want people to climb, plant a wild lime.

Wild Tamarind (*Lysiloma latisiliquum*)

Rare Wild Tamarind Is a Lollapalooza of a Native Tree

The wild tamarind (*Lysiloma latisiliquum*) is a lollapalooza of a native tree. Completing the tamarind trio are the Guatemalan and Bahamian tamarind. Do not confuse them with the African tamarind tree that has edible pulp around its seeds and is used in hot, spicy sauces, Caribbean sweets and Indian cooking. The edible variety can be found in the Audubon House garden. The name comes from *tamar* which means dried date and (h)*ind* which refers to India.

The wild tamarind tree's seeds are definitely not edible. They are much shorter, only four to five inches long, have a rather distinctive thin, brown and white pod that turns gradually to deep dark brown. It is flat, but sometimes twisted on the ends. Our native wild tamarind is quite rare in the Lower Keys, although it seeds readily. The seedpods make the same castanet sounds of other plants in the Fabaceae family.

Reaching fifty feet in height, the wild tamarind provides excellent shade. The trunk can grow to three feet in diameter and on older trees has a flat scaling bark. The bark is in strong contrast to its wispy, obovate (oval) leaves that look a lot like a poinciana tree except that the branches drape gracefully downward like a ballerina's limbs. If it is grown near a driveway or sidewalk, these tendrils should be trimmed. In fact, in order to produce a strong trunk the tree needs aggressive pruning of its lower branches while it is growing. All branches growing under ten feet should be removed.

Jack Kepler (www.renegadewood.com), a native tree woodworker likes this dark, rare wood because its interesting grains, similar to black walnut, reflect the light, changing from golden hues to brown. He has used the wood to carve a four poster bed and an entertainment center. Since this wood is protected from harvest, Kepler finds his wood after hurricanes and once found a forty-four inch wild tamarind with a thirty inch hole in the center. This fifty-year-old tree rotted when water got into its pith after a branch snapped off. Termites and carpenter ants had eaten the pith. Not one to waste the wood, he made coffee table bases from the circular wood.

Tiny, white puff balls cover the tree in the spring and on through the fall and are very fragrant. They attract much wildlife, from the cassius blue, large orange sulphur, and mimosa yellow butterflies to the native tree snails which affix themselves to the smooth bark of the young trees. These snails must conserve water during the dry months and to do so they create a watertight seal between the bark and themselves. Look for their brown and white shell with ringed stripes about head high and upwards on the trunk. Birds also like these trees, especially our migrating warblers.

Being a native, the sun-loving tree can grow in nutrient-poor, salty soil, and is drought and salt wing tolerant. If it is directly in salt winds, its leaves may burn, but they grow right back. The new young red leaves contrast with the light green of the older leaves. Few pests or diseases attack this native.

The State of Florida says that the wild tamarind has outstanding ornamental features and should be planted more in the Lower Keys because it is such a useful shade tree. It could be used in parking lots and as street plantings because its roots do not cause problems. As it is evergreen, it is an excellent specimen tree for yards or public parks.

There is a Wild Tamarind Trail at John Pennekamp Coral Reef State Park that is a twenty-minute walk through numerous native trees. The tree also can be seen in the driveway of 1800 Atlantic Blvd Condominiums. It grows quickly. You can buy one that is ten feet tall for $170 at MARC House.

If the wild tamarind is in tune with your tastes, it could play its castanets in your front yard.

Yellow Trumpet Tree (*Tabebuia aurea, heterophylla or rosea*)

Cha-cha in the Breeze with the Yellow Trumpet Tree

The prodigious flowers of the yellow trumpet tree flagrantly toss their windblown tresses like a blonde beauty who knows she's being admired. Who wouldn't admire the *Tabebuia aurea* when she is so flashy? Hanging around parking lots and street corners she slyly says, "Look at me, I am a very desirable tree. Wouldn't you like one of my sisters in your yard? Come and cha-cha with me in the breeze."

Topping out at twenty-five feet, Keys Energy finds her attractive as well, as she won't get near the power lines like the mahoganies, which have their boughs trimmed into silly Y shapes as a safety precaution.

The trumpet tree needs to be pruned into a single trunk to establish a strong central core or it breaks easily in strong winds. Its root system is shallow, so staking it is imperative until it is firmly established. Hurricanes scatter branches everywhere, but the tree comes back nicely. Its thin trunk has rough bark.

Yellow flowers in the shape of trumpets burst into bloom between the end of March and the end of April with trees next to each other flowering at the same time. Seeing a row of these blooming in a parking lot or down a street is spectacular. The tree is frequently shaped asymmetrically. The leaves drop and then the three-inch long yellow trumpet-shaped flowers emerge with inch-wide, flared mouths containing five ruffled-edged lobes with the texture of tissue paper. Two prominent ridges flow from the lower lobes into the throat of the flower.

The leaves are palmate, which means that they spread from a central core into five fingers. Terminal panicles can have leaves up to eleven inches long and one inch wide. They are green or silvery gray with tan fuzzy undersides. *Tabubuia* has a dense crown of golden panicles unless you water it too much, which reduces the number of blooms. Blooming at the end of the dry season when it has not rained for six weeks is perfect for this wench. Flowers may appear on older trees during the summer. If you have a sprinkling system, turn it off six weeks before its bloom period.

Seeds form in long, eight-inch capsules that are pointed on each end. They are gray-brown, glossy, and somewhat woody. They stay on the tree all winter. Propagation is from seed, air layering or grafting.

The yellow trumpet tree is relatively free of pests except for rare reports of leaf spot, dieback and spider mites. The one thing that can hurt this beauty is un-loving frost. She's a warm-hearted thing and if given the cold shoulder she withers and dies.

The yellow trumpet tree is native to the Caribbean, Central and South America. While not native to the Florida Keys it is not invasive either. Beloved in the springtime by nature lovers, it does well here. It likes our good drainage, alkaline soil and is drought tolerant once established. If planted in full sun, away from the salt breezes, it thrives and grows quickly.

This tree is a crucial resource for the Spix's macaw butterfly (*Cyanopsitta spixit*), which is extinct in the wild. However, approximately one hundred still exist in captivity. Before that species gets reintroduced into the wild, there must be plenty of *Tabubuia aurea* available for nesting.

The *T. aureas* has cousins with different coloration. The tall *T. rosea* which you see around Key West is light orchid. In all, there are over two hundred species in the Bignoniaceae family.

Putting this tropical golden girl in your yard or street side will guarantee some spring time smiles--a tree of gold that will bring you visual wealth.

Ylang-ylang tree *(Cananga odorata)*

Bo and Coco Create the Ideal Perfume

Earnest Bo was born in 1881 in Moscow into a famous perfume family that supplied the Russian Royalty. Then came the revolution! Bo moved to Paris and it was there that Coco Chanel gave him the job of creating a 'perfect' perfume for women. He presented Nos. 1-5 and 20 – 24, Coco chose No. 5. Chanel No. 5 was born in 1921. It is composed of rose, jasmine and ylang-ylang flower oils. When a reporter asked Marilyn Monroe what she wore to bed, she smiled in her seductive way and responded "Chanel No. 5" thereby supposedly making it, instantly, the most popular perfume in the world.

Ylang-ylang oil *(Cananga odorata)* it is produced in Indonesia and the Philippines. The tree can grow to one hundred feet in height and the fragrance of the all year long, night blooming blossoms is heady. The tree belongs to the Annonaceae family which includes sugar apple and soursop. In Tagalog, (Native Filipino language and he second most spoken Asian language in the US), 'alang-alang' means the flower of all flowers. The flowers are pollinated by night moths, therefore the smell is most fragrant in the evening. For use in perfume, the flowers are picked at dawn and put into a distillation process for fourteen hours. (Read the book *Perfume:The Story of a Murderer* by Patrick Suskind if you are interested in this process.)

The tree grows quickly but it takes three to four years before the tree produces flowers. Fruit, an oval one inch seed, and yellow flowers occur at the same time. The fruit tastes something like pine. The tree's branches droop and the dark, evergreen leaves come in pairs making it

58

shaped like a Christmas tree. There is a dwarf version, *(C.O. var. fruticosa)* that grows to only six feet and is suitable for potting   Flowers come right out of the branches, first emerging as curled green balls. As they ripen, they change from green to sharp yellow and drape down like a golden-haired movie star.

In the Philippines, there is a story of a childless couple to whom the gods granted a wish. They wished for a daughter and named her Llang. Of course, there were strings attached. Once she matured, the beautiful daughter could never touch a man. One day, when her parents were away, she went out in the gardens to pick a bouquet of flowers. A handsome young man who had secretly fallen in love with her beauty appeared and took her hand saying, "I love you. Be my wife." Instantly, the girl disappeared and turned into a ylang-ylang tree. The young man was heartbroken and wandered the magic garden for all eternity calling her name.

The flower is made into leis, purportedly rubbed on the scalp to promote hair growth and as a salve for insect stings and snake bites. At one time, the fragrance was sprayed on winter coats before they went into summer storage. The oil is reputed to scare away malicious spirits and, as an aphrodisiac, heighten a woman's sexual appeal.

'Aqua De Gio' by Armani 'Poison' by Dior and 'Elise Fields' by Guerlain contain the ylang-ylang scent. It is often used by aroma therapists and masseuses to relieve stress.

Ylang-ylang can be fifteen feet in width so plan appropriately. It requires no special pruning, its roots are non-invasive, it has no pest problems and it can take a strong wind. Plant it in full sun and it will bloom year round and smell wonderful. Ylang-ylang thrives in our high humidity. You can see this tree by the Orchid Room at the Key West Garden Club.

SHRUBS

American Beautyberry (*Callicarpa Americana*)

Birds Love the American Beautyberry

Agricultural Research Scientist Charles T. Byronson's Mississippi grandfather used to pull off a branch of the beautyberry bush, crush the fuzzy leaves and put them in the harness of his draft animals to keep flies, mosquitoes and ticks away. Folks in his neighborhood mashed the leaves for the aromatic oil and rubbed it on their skins. He told the U.S. Agricultural Service about his granddaddy's remedy and three insect–repelling compounds were successfully extracted from beautyberry and patented. This folk remedy investigation resulted in the discovery of natural repellants that are as powerful as DEET. (*Science Daily*, Feb. 2, 2006)

If you have the space, (8' X 8') you, too, can have beautyberry (*Callicarpa americana*, Verbenaceae family) growing in your own yard! (Keys Energy gave them away this year.) Plop it in the full sun for best results, or slide it into some light shade. It's evergreen, coarse, two- to six- inch long leaves form a bushy shrub. With a little organic material or mulch you'll get a big plant, but beautyberry grows quickly in our nutrient-poor soils as well. If it is not planted right on the beach, it is salt, wind and water tolerant. As it is drought tolerant, it is good for xeriscaping.

The pale pink flowers of the beautyberry grow right next to the stem and are insignificant. The reason that it is called a beauty is because of the lavish production of neon magenta and violet berries packed tightly on its stems. Deer love these berries. Mockingbirds, brown thrashers, catbirds, and towhees can strip the bush in days. I've heard stories of robins getting drunk on the berries, falling off the branches and staggering around under the bush. This could be excellent "Birds Behaving Badly" watching! Seeds are spread by the birds and you might find this bush popping up under other taller trees. If you don't get new bushes you can easily propagate them by taking softwood cuttings, putting them in sand and keeping them moist.

Prune this bush aggressively in the early spring if it gets lanky, as it only gets flowers and fruit on new growth. It should be thinned carefully so that any flowers or seeds are not removed. Use it as a broad border plant or underneath taller trees. It is a good foundation plant. Three planted together make a powerful statement.

Beautyberry is a maintenance-free plant and has no major diseases or root problems. The caterpillars of a moth, (*Endoclita malabaricus*) may occasionally chew off the leaves. Examples of the plant can be found in the Key West Garden Club at West Martello. Beautyberry is readily available in nurseries at a low price.

I hope you beautyberry gardeners try using these plant's leaves to repel no-see-ums and report back to this author with the results.

Bay Cedar *(Suriana maritima)*

Tough Bay Cedar Is on Florida's Threatened List

When I am older, I yearn to be that old woman I've named Arleen who I see riding her rusting, conch cruiser down the Key West streets. Strong, supple and straight, she has survived a long life with her spine and her dignity intact. The bay cedar *(Suriana maritima)* is that kind of plant. She can take the worst of it. Send her a hurricane and she laughs. Put her in the blazing sun and she thrives. Salt wind or salt water doesn't faze her. She eats our nutrient-poor, alkaline, sandy soil with gusto. With these abilities you'd think that there would be many of her around, but she is listed as threatened by the State of Florida, not because she is delicate, but because rapid building on the shoreline has destroyed much of her native habitat.

She can grow up to twenty feet tall and ten feet wide, but typically is only ten by six. Her tiny evergreen leaves vary from dark green to green-gray and create a densely-leaved bush. Leaves and twigs are covered with soft down when they emerge. Tiny yellow flowers bloom year round, followed by small brown seeds surrounded by a five-pointed ring of sepals. She's a traveler like my favorite old woman, Arleen. She gets around on the sea as her seeds float and survive for long periods in salt water, which is why they pop up on tropical beaches all over the world.

Not only can this shrub survive and prosper in the most inclement climate on beaches, it can also be grown in pots on balconies without getting wind damaged. It can be clipped into a superior hedge and is so sturdy it even can be used around parking lots or on median strips in the highway. The shrubs can be trimmed to be a vertical wall around a fence or made into a tree. The branches smell like cedar and would grace any parlor in a flower arrangement.

Key deer are respectful and do not nibble on her leaves, but birds feed on her generous proliferation of seeds. Blue, martial scrub hairstreak and mallow scrub hairstreak butterfly larvae dote on her leaves. The great southern whites, Julias, obscure skippers and others share her potent blossom nectar with bees and wasps. Herbalists use extracts of her leaves and bark to treat rheumatism, skin ulcers and to stop hemorrhaging.

You can see a three-foot example out at Ft. Zachary Taylor and a six-foot one along the fence in front of 1609 Patricia Street.

This plant can be grown from seed but since it grows so slowly you might prefer to start with a larger plant. Nursery prices are $20 for a three-gallon plant. She is a slow grower, but with little care, she will be strong and supple for a long time. Take Arleen home with you.

Bahama Cassia *(Senna Mexicana var. chapmanii)*

Golden Treasure in Your Garden

While treasure hunters look for gold under the ocean, gardeners find it easily in the yellow flowers of the Bahama Cassia (*Senna Mexicana* var. *chapmanii*.) This shrub blooms profusely, attracting insects, bees and magnificent, yellow sulphur butterflies whose caterpillars are eaten by birds. This is a full treasure chest of native landscaping.

This robust, leggy Countess waves her golden treasure in the breeze. She can fill a large space (8' X 8') in the landscape and look regal when planted in groupings. The plant only lasts five or six years, but it self-seeds and new sprouts come up under the older plants. The evergreen leaves are two inches long and alternate on branching stems. They are a fine, airy green topped off with flowers that look like golden crowns. The plant is in the pea and bean family (Leguminosae) so the clutch of flowers looks like a handful of sweet peas. Seeds and flowers form primarily in the fall and winter, but mine have been in flower all year. The plentiful seeds are encased in elongated seed packets that dry to dark brown. They will self-start all over the garden. Cassias grow in light shade or full sun.

Countess *Cassia* is native so she tolerates drought, salt water and salt wind. She gets an 8/10 rating for hurricane tolerance from D'Asign Source in its *Keynoter* "Hurricane Landscape Guide." Greedily she pulls nutritional gold from the poorest of sandy, alkaline soils as long as they are well-drained. For thick luxuriant growth prune one-third of her yearly. Give her lots of space.

64

She makes an impressive specimen plant, such as the one at 1800 Atlantic Boulevard near the bicycle path. She also would be good as a loose border or to fill a large area or in front of a fence. She is especially beautiful looking down from a second floor window. The State of Florida Agricultural Services recommends she be planted more frequently. She has a big family, so be careful that you are getting exactly what you want when you buy it. Some *cassias* are trees and some are groundcovers.

Sulphur butterfly larvae feed on this plant, so not only does it enrich your yard with flowers on the plant, it looks like the flowers are walking on air as the yellow butterflies spiral and soar across its blossoms as if performing for royalty. It attracts orange barred sulphur, cloudless sulphur, Mexican yellow and many other butterflies. Look for their small oval eggs on the flower buds.

Once you plant Countess *Cassia*, you can propagate more royalty from her seeds or transplant the ones that pop up in your garden. From seed to large bush takes under a year.

Bahama Coffee (*Psychotria ligustrifolia*), Wild Coffee (*Psychotria nervosa*), Velvetleaf Wild Coffee (*Psychotria sulzner*)

Wild Birds Invade Wild Coffees

Watch the birds go wild at the taste of your landscape if you plant a native, endangered wild coffee. It's a way of "going green" in the garden. In the Florida Keys, native plants often get overlooked when homeowners plant colorful exotic gardens. Because they are so easy to maintain and so good for our wildlife, they deserve to be considered as first choice plants.

Once established, the fuss-free coffees need little water—a perfect addition to a xeriscape landscape. They traditionally grow in the under story of hardwood hammocks where their foliage creates a rich green color in the shaded areas in which they thrive. Too much sunlight makes their leaves turn yellow. These shrubs can grow to ten feet, but take to trimming well and can be kept at whatever height the homeowner desires, even as a small tree. The round bushes spread from four to eight feet. They have showy white flowers in spring and summer and then a proliferation of fleshy, red, drive-the-birds-crazy fruits.

There are three varieties: Bahama coffee (*Psychotria ligustrifolia*), wild coffee (*Psychotria nervosa*), and the seldom-found velvetleaf wild coffee (*Psychotria sulzneri*). They come from the

66

Rubiaceae family and one South American variety does have psycho-active compounds, hence the name. You can tell them apart by their four- to eight-inch leaves. Bahama coffee has glossy green leaves. Wild coffee has puckered, markedly veined, glossy leaves that glint and glimmer as light reflects off of them. Velvetleaf wild coffee has deep blue-green, velvety leaves. They are green year round so look good in a mass planting.

Native plants like the coffees increase the diversity of natural insect predators and attract other types of sought-after wildlife species such as bees, butterflies and the voracious cardinals and blue jays. Joyfully, no serious pests or diseases attack them. People used to brew coffee from the seeds which resulted in a drink with no caffeine.

Coffees are incredibly resilient plants. They love our alkaline, limestone soils, well-drained and sandy. They grow near saltwater and can take the wind or a short flood, and even a bit of drought. Since they are so happy in the Keys landscape, they grow moderately fast without much attention. Put them someplace where they can get ten feet tall and you'll never have to trim them.

These plants are good as informal hedges, buffer plantings around a foundation, or as accent shrubs. They would be good planted as background with some blanket flower (*Gaillardia*) in front of them or to create a sight barrier. They would be splendid outside a window where you could watch the greedy cardinals and blue jays gorge on the berries.

You get additional green points in your garden for planting these natives which are listed as endangered by the State of Florida. The cost is low. A three-gallon Bahama or wild coffee was $5 when I checked a Homestead nursery. If you want to add a little pizzazz to your shade garden, the native, endangered coffees are an impressive and inexpensive plant.

Firebush *(Hamelia patens)*

The Firebush Is Hot, Hot, Hot

In those dog days of August, when it's just too much work for most flowers to even think about blooming, the reliable firebush cries "Bring on the Bikram. Pour on the heat!" The hotter and dryer the weather, the brighter the reddish-orange flowers bloom. Good growing conditions for the firebush would dry out weeds.

This native perennial is a member of the Rubiaceae family, like the ever-flowering *Ixoras* and *Pentas*. It has multiple, tubular flowers that are an inch and a half long. They fork out from the tips of the branches all year long blooming in the middle of the night and wilting by the end of the next day. Flowers must be pollinated quickly in order to produce a seed. The iridescent-green halicted bee, Pluto sphinx moth and the statira sulphur and black swallowtail butterflies and hummingbirds love these flowers. A plethora of half-inch seeds start out red, turn black and hang in clusters from the ends of the branches. They are edible and taste slightly acidic, but they make your mouth feel fuzzy so I wouldn't advise trying them. They can be fermented into an alcoholic drink. The plant both seeds and flowers at the same time and creates a feast for mockingbirds and catbirds.

The branches break easily. Leaves whorl in groups of three and are four to eight inches long. They turn brilliant red as they age. The stems and veins are red. In sun it creates dense foliage, in shade it becomes leggy and does not flower as much. It grows in well-drained, poor nutrient soil, xeriscaping at its best. Don't bother fertilizing.

Indigenous people in tropical America used the leaves and stems in tanning hides. Crushed leaves were applied to cuts and bruises. Adding vinegar to the crushed leaves relieved rashes and insect stings. The plant was used as a deodorant and as a cure for dysentery. The medical world is examining it for its anti-bacterial and anti-fungal properties.

This bush is also known as scarlet bush, hummingbird bush, *xkana, chichipin, zorrillo real, sisipinse, uvero, paanete* and…the list goes on. That's why botanists invented scientific names. The genus *Hamilia* was named in honor of Henry Louis Duhamel du Monceau, an important 18th century French botanist. *Patens* means spreading out flat and the bush does so easily. One bush puts out seeds enough to fill an entire yard with twelve by eight foot bushes.

It can be grown as a hedge, screen or accent border. It looks good in a mass planting. It grows well in a pot on the patio. You compulsive whackers will love trimming this bush as it prunes easily and grows back quickly. It can be cut right to the ground and will grow back. Hurricane Wilma totally destroyed these bushes and they were the first things to return.

The State of Florida recommends firebush as having outstanding ornamental value and recommends that it should be planted more. (When buying, don't mistake this giant for the smaller African firebush which is invasive. It has yellowish red flowers and hairless leaves.) Expect to pay around $8.

Jamaican Caper (*Capparis cynophallophora*)

The Fecund Jamaican Caper Relies on Perfect Flowers

The Jamaica caper (*Capparis cynophallophora*) is a widely popular large shrub or tree that emits a nightly fragrance that will stop a sensitive human in a heartbeat. The three-inch, brush-like flowers start out white and turn deep maroon within a few hours. A white, four-petaled flower forms the base. It is called perfect in the botanical world because male and female parts are found on the same flower. Alec Bristow in *The Sex Life of Plants* states that plants invented sex long before the first animals appeared, and when plants invented sex, they also invented beauty.

This hermaphrodite in the Capparaceae family has an unusual anatomy. Remember your high school botany? The caper's orange tipped female pistil is longer than the male stamens which have the pollen grains. The pollen-filled anthers on purple stamens droop dejectedly far beneath the tubes they need to enter. How does the pollen reach the end of the pistil tube? The showy flowers start blooming in April and attract a myriad of insects, bees, and butterflies, and lizards. Even the wind gets to flirt with moving that pollen. Somehow, with their help, the caper gets pregnant.

Immediately after pollination, the male anthers wilt. The seed pods begin to form in the rainy season and grow to as much as ten inches long. These truly amazing seed pods burst open and contain brilliant orange-red, sticky pulp around the seeds. It is Christmas in September for the birds, with the red seedpods dangling from the branches like ornaments. I observed two doves and a rare white-crowned pigeon precariously balanced on the thin branches, contorting their bodies to reach the pulpy plunder. The messy birds get it all over their feathers. Pulp that drops on the ground gets devoured by ants. (The Jamaican caper seed is related to the edible caper served in salads, but it is not edible.)

Delicate, pastel-bronze leaves are folded together when they emerge. As they mature, these three-inch, evergreen leaves turn dark, shiny green on the top and a shimmering rust color on the bottom. You can identify the oval leaf because it has a little dimple at the tip. The dense leaves rustle, softly singing in the breeze.

Thin branches encourage its use by small wildlife. Dense foliage turns the Jamaican caper into an excellent barrier to hide an unpleasant view or create privacy. It is sturdy and can take being planted along highways. It would be lovely in a spot that gets foot traffic in the evening to take advantage of the fragrance of its flowers. It can be pruned into a tree by cutting off the lower branches or be cut as a hedge.

Its showy flowers and seeds turn this shrub into a specimen plant for the yard. The fifteen foot native is a hurricane survivor. Drought, salt soil and salt wind tolerant, it grows with poor nutrition in our alkaline, sandy soil. Seedlings pop up under the branches and transplant well, but grow slowly without fertilizer. Direct sun will produce the fastest growth. For a less dense, open look, put it in the shade.

No serious pests or diseases attack this Keys native. It can be propagated by scarified seeds. Often there are seedlings under the branches of the trees that can be transplanted. It is readily available in nurseries and should cost around $15.

An example of the Jamaican Caper can be seen at the Key West Garden Club.

Jatropha (Jatropha integerrima)

Jatropha Tree Is a Bio-fuel Extraordinaire

Apparently, the *Jatropha* is the hottest tree to hit the bio-diesel fuel market ever. One cultivar, the *J. curcas* is being planted at lightening speed in China, India, Brazil, Gambia, Nicaragua, Tanzania, Mali, Kenya, Costa Rica and of course, California. In the future, we may not be *selling* as much as we are *buying* from Cuba, where the *Jatropha* tree is native.

This amazing tree can be propagated by seed or cutting a branch off of the tree and sticking it in the ground. Africans make natural fences around their compounds from these bushes to keep animals out as the leaves and stems are toxic, something to note if you have a deer or iguana problem. A tree's seeds can be harvested after only eighteen months. It will live for fifty years and produce seeds to be harvested twice a year.

The State of Florida has given twenty-five million dollars in "Farm to Fuel" grants to farmers to grow these trees. They can be intercropped with sugar cane, fruit trees, coffee bushes or even vegetables. Large nursery plantings and micro-credit loans to women are fueling the production in India. *Jatropha* trees line the route of the train that runs from Mumbai to Delhi. The train runs on 20% *Jatropha* oil.

Processing this bio-fuel is as easy as making olive oil. Electricity is not needed to make the oil. Shell the seeds, press them and you have fuel that can go directly into a diesel fuel tank. Anyone from natives in the Zimbabwean bush to industrial farms can make this. One acre can produce 600 to 1,000 gallons of oil. The residue can be used to make soap, cosmetics, tannins, dyes, lantern fuel and candles. This oil even kills snails. A Mexican company has developed a fertilizer that increases corn growth 880%. No wonder the world is planting acres of these bushy trees.

The species that we see here in Key West is the *Jatropha integerrima,* from the Euphorbiaceae (spurge) family. It is also called peregrine or spicy jatropha. The name comes from the Greek word *iatros* which means physician, and the word *trophe* which means nutrition. Two other common names are psychic nut or doctor food.

The *Jatropha* is a small tree, ten to fifteen feet tall. The leaves begin as bronze beauties. Once mature they are dark green on top and brown on the bottom. They are shaped in a variety of patterns. One is a single, long, oval, pointed leaf: another has three prominent lobes; a third is elliptically or fiddle shaped. The sap is a skin irritant and the seeds are poisonous if eaten raw.

It can be a bush or, if trimmed, a tree. Pruning makes it get bushier and it can be pruned any time of the year. Male and female flowers exist on the same tree. The flowers form clusters of five-pointed, inch long, scarlet blossoms with a yellow center shaped like a star. Year round, blossoms on thin stems pop up and down in the breeze.

The *Jatropha* is a scrub wasteland plant in Cuba. It likes the hot, dry, sunny days and as long as the soil drains well, it is not particular about where it grows. It's resistant to drought and pests. Use it as a shrub, a fence, as a potted, patio plant or as a specimen tree.

The flowers attract monarch, swallow tail and zebra butterflies, so this is a good plant to fill your garden with those flutter-bys. Hummingbirds are also fond of them.

Do you remember Friar Lawrence's admonishment to Romeo while contemplating a plant from the garden? "Poison hath residence, and medicine power." So the *Jatropha* has both poison and power. Let's hope the power part of this winner takes off and supplies us with home grown bio fuel.

Locustberry (*Byrsonima lucida*)

Locustberry Flirts with Its Ruffled Petticoats

It's Spring! It's Spring! And nothing declares it like the luscious native shrub, locustberry (*Byrsonima lucida*). Flowers are *everywhere* on this harbinger of spring. They don't mind changing their outfits as they get older, going from virginal white when they first emerge through precocious pink to a passionate, scarlet red as they reach maturity. One floral cluster can have the entire range of colors punctuated with tiny yellow stamens. Locustberry is endangered and the State of Florida recommends planting it more. How could we resist planting the ruffled petticoats of this princess? Her Malpighia family doesn't mind.

The shiny leaves are small at the stem and rounded at the ends. They can change color too. Due to the oil glands, the underside of the leaf changes from green to yellow. The bush is multi-trunked and usually forms a round, twelve foot plant, as tall as it is broad. However, it can remain as small as one foot high or get as tall as thirty-five feet high depending on the characteristics of the seed that is planted and the soil in which it grows. Its growth rate is moderate and it stays green year round.

Byrsonima means tanning in Greek. The bark was once used for tanning hides. *Lucida* means shining, in reference to the plants' shiny leaves. The edible, round green seeds turn red-brown as they age. They stay attached as perfect food for wildlife.

As a Keys native, this flouncing flirt can take full sun. She loves our well-drained, sandy soils and if it doesn't rain, she doesn't care. She should be planted away from the ocean front as salt wind can burn her leaves. She can take a bit of a flood and survived Hurricane Wilma just dandy.

The plant is a larval and nectar host plant for the Florida duskywing butterfly, (*Ephyriades brunnea*). The light green larvae protect themselves from predators by weaving a few leaves together with silken threads. After metamorphosis, the butterflies feed on the flower nectar.

She attracts insects that like to sip the nectar of her flowers which in turn attract migrating warblers, vireos and flycatchers that devour these crunchy insects. Cardinals and white-eyed vireos like to nest in her thick foliage. Mockingbirds stuff her fruits into their offspring's open beaks.

No root problems, not affected by pests or diseases, she's a peachy plant who needs no tending. Plant her where there is a lot of space as a border or a hedge. A three-gallon locustberry, 24 inches high, can be had for $8.50 and a seven-gallon, 36" goes for $35 in a Homestead Nursery.

This sweetheart, locustberry, can be seen in the wild, blooming on Key Deer Boulevard on Big Pine Key and between the tennis courts at 1800 Atlantic Boulevard, Key West.

Wait until you see her petticoats in the spring!

Rosemary (Rosmarinus officianlis)

Think Outside the Pot:
Grow Rosemary as an Aromatic Shrub

One of my most memorable aroma moments occurred in California walking up a path toward a house in Silver Lake. As I brushed the dense shrubs, the aroma wafted to my nostrils and I realized that I was engulfed in a sea of rosemary.

As a result of that heady experience, I ask you to re-examine rosemary as more than an herb grown in small pots on the patio. Think of it as a robust bush that can grow to six feet tall and four feet wide or be clipped to a small hedge. It should be included in your sunny landscaping plans for the pleasure of using it in your culinary arts as well as providing your dinner guests with a remarkable experience as they brush through it to your door.

Rosemary (*Rosmarinus officainlis*) a native of the Mediterranean area, is a stiff erect bush whose skinny leaves are green on the top and silver on the bottom. It's a woody member of the mint family (Larniaceae). There are twenty-four types of upright rosemary and another twelve types of creeping rosemary *(R. prostrates.)* A tiny, pale blue, trumpet-shaped flower forms on the tip of a young shoot in the spring. Other varieties have white, pink or violet flowers that you can toss in your salad. It loves to have its roots dry and its leaves damp in our high humidity. It can withstand poor sandy soil, drought tolerant dry roots, high humidity--no wonder it thrives here.

Rosemary has quite a history. Sumerians wrote about it on their cuneiform tablets. The Egyptians burned it in sick rooms as a disinfectant and to ward off the plague. Pharaohs took it with them to the next world. In Christian lore, Mary threw her cloak over the rosemary bush when she was resting on her flight to Egypt. When she removed it, the flowers had turned from white to blue. Rosemary grew on the Gallipoli battlefield on the Turkish coast in WW I and soldiers fought among its perfumed leaves. It has been used in wedding bouquets, baptisms, funerals and as an herb of remembrance, perhaps because its smell is so memorable.

In *Romeo and Juliet*, (Act IV, Sc. 5) Friar Laurence tells the nurse upon Juliet's feigned death, "Dry up your tears and stick your rosemary / On this fair corpse, and as the custom is. / And in her best array bear her to church; / For though fond nature bids us all lament, / Yet nature's tears are reason's merriment." thereby using rosemary for both the death and the rebirth of Juliet.

Propagation is easy. Clip off a short branch, dip it in root hormone and put it in a pot with good drainage. Soon you will have a new plant. Don't worry about cutting branches off the bush as it grows even thicker when trimmed. If you trim a lot of it off, the smell may require that you head immediately for your kitchen to start those rosemary potatoes or roasted chicken. Or you could throw branches on the coals while grilling for a sensation both aromatic and tasty.

You can bonsai these plants either in the ground or in a pot. They can even become topiary if you have the patience. I'm thinking of a topiary rosemary flamingo on the lawn. If you would like a long stem, simply cut off all of the branches on the trunk and leave a pom-pom on the top. Rosemary needs at least six hours of sun a day.

Small rosemary Christmas trees are often sold in winter. My Christmas tree rosemary plant dried out and died very quickly. Rosemary has tiny shallow hair-like roots which like water and good drainage. It should not be allowed to dry out. This doesn't happen when it is planted in the ground...but in a small pot the watering is more difficult to control. Water every two to three days and let the water drain through the pot. Powdery mildew can be a problem if rosemary gets too wet.

Aromatic rosemary oil is used as an insect repellant and in massage therapy to increase blood flow just below the skin surface. I have an eye pillow that is filled with fragrant rosemary flowers. Bees enjoy the flowers and insects do not attack the bush, probably because they do not like its smell. It is readily available in local stores.

Sea Lavender (*Argusia gnaphalodes*)

Sea Lavender Tosses Her Gray Locks in the Salt Wind

An elderly lady in lavender inhabits our beaches, perched on a blanket of sand with her gray hair in an unwavering coif. She looks like she has lived there all of her life, but in fact, the scientific name for sea lavender, *Argusia,* refers to the Argun River found on the border between Manchuria and Russia. *Gnaphalodes* refers to a family of cudweed. The word comes from the Greek and means lock of wool. The bush resembles a larger version of rosemary. Her family, Boraginaceae, is respectful of the old lady, being the forget-me-not family.

Despite her foreign genealogy, she is native to the Florida Keys and state-listed as endangered. She's difficult to propagate, despite the dispersal of her corky, brown seeds via ocean waves. The website www.regionalconservation.org states that "massive numbers of new plants may recruit after a storm if seeds are present." I have not seen that happen on our beaches. Some sources report good luck with cuttings, but it takes at least six weeks. Much of her habitat has been destroyed by developers or eroded by waves. Her old neighborhood is gone, but in Key West she has been replanted by the city on the beaches.

The Garden Club's three-foot by eight-foot plant was in the direct spray from waves and got the brunt of tropical storm Ike's salt wind, survived. Her leaves filled with water as though she had gotten a rejuvenating treatment at the spa. Sea lavender is a sultry gray-green and has narrow, thick, hairy leaves growing in a shape a bit like a pom-pom chrysanthemum. The fuzzy leaves slow the loss of water, protecting them from strong solar radiation. They grow to about one and one-half inches directly on a long trunk. Old leaves often hang on to the trunk long after shriveling up.

She likes salty soil, and grows well but slowly in the secondary dunes on the beach. Her roots find the water a few feet below her. She is content with that and needs no supplemental watering. However, well-drained sandy, nutrient-poor soil is her milieu, so don't plant her where water accumulates or she will soon be afflicted with diseases. As long as she is on the dunes she is pest and disease free, but she requires full sun to be happy.

The tight group of small white flowers is semi-showy against the ever gray-green leaves. The petals curl back tightly to expose a yellow-brown center. The bottommost flowers open first. The white-to-mauve flowers attract pollinating insects and are nectar plants for butterflies. The small round seeds form on these same stems.

Fishermen brewed up a black tea from the leaves and the plant has been reportedly used in abortions and to treat venereal disease.

You can see this plant at the Key West Garden Club in the native section or in the wild on the beach at Berg Bird Preserve at 1700 Atlantic Blvd. This plant is available at native nurseries but it is relatively expensive, with a one-gallon specimen going for $25.

Sea lavender is in eminent danger of extirpation (extinction) so treat the lady with respect and admiration when you see her gray head relaxing on the beaches.

Thryallis (*Galphimia glauca*)

Key West Garden Club Propagates Deer Proof Thryallis

The Key West Garden Club's propagation section is outside of the actual fort and seldom is seen by the public. Nevertheless, it is the heartbeat of the Garden Club. It is where plants are grown from cuttings, seeds or seedlings. Garden Club members are always on the lookout for young plants that spring up as seedlings around older varieties and collecting seeds from strong desirable natives.

In charge of this beehive of activity s Kitty Somerville, with her cast of many players. "Oooo, look at how this ambrosia has grown," or "The frangipani has flowered red!" can be heard in the small area as the volunteers arrive and begin their first task, weeding.

When I arrived one Monday morning, Kitty was giving her weekly plant lecture on thryallis, (*Galphimia glauca*). Thryallis was a big seller at the last garden sale because deer will *not* eat it. Not so important in Key West, but critical on Pig Pine and Summerland. She brought in cuttings from one of her personal plants containing small dark seeds. From underneath the plant she had dug up seedlings. As she explained the characteristics of the plants to the volunteers, they gathered together the materials that they needed to propagate the shrub.

Thryallis is a fast-growing evergreen shrub that matures at about six feet tall and five feet wide. Although a native to Mexico and Central America, it grows well in South Florida, at the tip of Texas and along the coast of California and it is not invasive here. It blooms year round in our sub-tropical climate with bright yellow flowers forming clusters on the tips of its branches. Rain of gold, golden shower and *noches buena* are some of its nicknames.

Its round, full form sports light green oblong leaves that are thin but a bit leathery and grow from reddish stems. The leaves have uses in traditional Latin American medicine for coronary problems, diarrhea, and stress. In Western medicine it is used primarily in pharmaceuticals to prevent allergies and asthma.

The Keys landscapers love this show-off because of its xeriscaping attributes. It is drought tolerant, loves the bright sun and tolerates poor, salty soil and has few diseases or pests. Plant it in a well drained area because its roots will rot if it is over watered.

Sheer it into a low hedge, but because it's smothered in blossoms year round they will be cut off with pruning. Remember to keep the bottom of the hedge wider than the top so that the lower leaves get plenty of sunshine. It is often used as a foundation plant, a background for shorter plants, in mass plantings or even formed into a topiary shape. It can be pruned into a small multi-legged tree. Place it in a pot and it will brighten your sunny balcony. If it gets too leggy, prune it in the winter and new growth will quickly ensue. Bees, caterpillars, butterflies and birds find reasons to come visiting the golden thryallis.

Kitty and her cohorts used a drop of Superthrive on the cuttings and planted them after dipping them in a root hormone to prevent fungus infections. They potted the seedlings, three to a six-inch pot and, in smaller pots, planted twenty-one seeds, again three to a pot.

Then the hardest activity for a gardener came, waiting patiently and watering the seemingly inert pots. In a few weeks, the propagation volunteers will say, "Look! Somebody's thryallis is up."

Yellow Necklace Pod (*Sophora tomentosa var. truncata*)

Yellow Necklace Pod Sails to Sandy Shores

Old salts who hang around the shores of islands like Key West, often meet up with their plant counterpart, the native shrub yellow necklace pod, (*Sophora tomentosa* var. *truncata*.) The plant starts out like a young sailor, all wonderfully fuzzy, silvery-green, and full of the juices of life. As he ages, his oval leaves lose their protective velvet and turn a bright green suitable for a bold sailor's life.

A bright yellow flower spike that could be as tall as sixteen inches pokes its flag into the sky from the terminal branch, screaming abundance to any passing wildlife. The pea-shaped flowers begin opening at the base and continue to the elongated tip.

Then seeds are produced. These six- to fifteen-inch long, green seed pods dry and shrink around the seeds as they turn brown like a necklace of dark pearls drawn from some sunken treasure chest. Plant them and they grow readily, but don't eat them as they induce violent vomiting. This evergreen plant flowers and seeds all year long. Necklace pod grows to ten feet tall and just as wide.

The scientific name *Sophora* comes from Arabic and means yellow. *Tomentosa* means densely woolly and *truncata* means cut off at the end. It's in the Luguminosae family of peas and beans and has a symbiotic relationship with the soil, producing nitrogen fixing bacteria. That means it is good for the sandy, alkaline soil in which it grows. There are no pests or diseases to mess with this old salt. It likes the full sun but can grow in partial shade. Like a sailor, it loves the salt wind. Once established it does not need watering, although you may hear it softly crooning "Yo, Ho, Ho, and a bottle of Conch Republic rum." Xeriscaping with natives is easy on the water bills.

This stunning Key West plant with an interesting texture can be a specimen plant in a showy place in your garden or as a loose natural hedge. It prefers natural trimming so don't chop it with a hedge trimmer. I've seen two excellent specimens against an outside fence on the 1600 block of Patricia Street in Key West. With the right pruning it can become a small tree with an interesting trunk. The University of Florida's Agricultural Extension Service says it has "outstanding ornamental features, and should be planted more."

Necklace pod leaves host the caterpillars of sulphur butterflies. Butterflies flutter by frequently and bees and wasps buzz by for a drink at its nectar bar. It is irresistible to the migrating ruby-throated hummingbirds that hover over its vibrant blossoms. The yellow-throated warbler is a frequent guest. What with the flapping of the wings, the buzzing of the bees and the chirping of the birds, it may sound like the old sailor is warbling the sea shanty, "What shall we do with the drunken sailor?"

Although not threatened, this plant is difficult to find at nurseries, but it is inexpensive when you do, $7.50 for a three-gallon plant.

VINES

Hoya (*Hoya carnosa*)

Margaret Nygren holding rooted hoya

Propagating Hoya

Ahoya the *Hoya*! Your grandma's wax plant has been passed down through generations and could be as old as the wandering Ancient Mariner. If you want to give a bit of history to your children or grandchildren, or maybe solidify a friendship, this is the plant that keeps on giving. It works well in pots or in the ground, as the vines twine up or cascade down. It will grow up a frame or a tree trunk. Although it is from Southeast Asia, The University of Florida recommends that it be grown more in the Florida Keys.

The *Hoya* (*Hoya carnosa*) was named after Thomas Hoy, the intelligent and successful 18th century gardener to the Duke of Northumberland. It was the star at the Garden Club's Monday morning lesson given by Kitty Somerville, assisted by Margaret Nygren. You want to grow this carefree vine because the long-lasting pink and white star-shaped flowers look like wax or porcelain. They are made up of twelve to sixteen small blossoms that are three inches wide and smell like chocolate. They bloom for two weeks at a time all summer long.

Three of the over two hundred species of evergreen, thick-leafed *Hoya* were on the potting bench at West Martello Fort--a variegated, a solid and a krinkle kurl. The *Hoya* has few seeds and they don't grow true to the original plant, so propagation is the best way to reproduce the plant.

First, sterilize everything. Make a solution of 10% bleach and water and dip the pots in the solution. Wipe your clippers with alcohol. Latex gloves while handling will keep your plant sterile and your nails clean. Then cut a section off of the grandmother plant at a 45 degree angle and strip the leaves, leaving two or three nodes on the stem and dip it in a root enzyme.

Put three or four small pieces into a pot that is full of wet soil—one third perlite, one third vermiculite and one third peat moss or half sand and perlite. A standard professional potting mix also works. Let the soil dry out completely before watering to avoid pest and disease problems. You don't want mealy bugs or spider mites.

It is in the Milkweed family so bees, ants, butterflies and hummingbirds love the flowers. Warning to gardeners: the flowers drip nectar, so don't hang this plant over a surface that requires cleaning unless you *enjoy* cleaning up messes. The vine likes indirect sunlight and does well under the overhang of a house or balcony where it can get lots of moving air. If the leaves turn yellow, it is getting too much sun. *Hoya* is similar to orchids and has been known to grow without soil in the crotch of a tree. Never prune the flower spurs off, as the plant blooms on the old wood as well as new shoots. Like the Mariner, they have a reputation for not blooming until they are old, so be patient.

Rosi Ware, Karen Conteras, Annette Liggett, Kathy Russ and Kitty Somerville propagating *Hoya*.

Passionflower (*Passiflora incarnata*)

Passionflower from Outer Space Takes over the Trellis

During my youth in Nebraska, I had to truck my ten-year-old body eight blocks to get from school to home. Being an adventurous girl, one merry May Day I decided to take a short cut across several vacant lots. Old foundations of houses long since demolished cluttered my path. Suddenly, an incredible flower popped up at my feet and stopped my progress like a purple stop light in my uncharted road.

I had picked flowers from my mother's garden to distribute to the neighbors on May Day, so I was experienced with irises, tulips, jonquils and dandelions, but I had never seen a flower so complicated. It should be in a conservatory with "Rare Bloom" posted on its sign. I thought it might be from outer space. On Saturday, I led my mother over to the lot and pointed out the vine which now had three flowers.

"That's a Maypop," she said. "It's also called a passionflower." It was a lesson from nature on the diversity and beauty in what mother called, "a weed that pops up in May." People are still arguing over whether the passionflower (*Passiflora incarnata*) is an invasive weed or a desirable arbor-covering vine. There are many cultivars of this vine. In the Florida Keys, this one is native and desired as a climbing vine with tendrils.

According to legend, it got its name, because the elaborate floral structure of a passion flower is similar to the elements of the Passion or Crucifixion of Christ: The five petals and five sepals are the ten Apostles (conveniently omitting Peter and Judas). The three pistils (or styles) are the nails of the Cross; The corona (or filaments) at the top of the flower is the Crown of Thorns, The five anthers are the five wounds. The stemmed ovary represents the chalice. On the other hand, one internet blogger said, "I cannot imagine an uglier flower."

This flower is never in arrangements because it only lives one day and then closes up to begin its journey towards forming a large, round, yellow edible fruit. It tastes sweet and acidic. People use it to make jellies, syrups, pies, cakes and ice cream. The juice, frozen in ice cube trays adds a snappy flavor to iced tea.

Three native butterflies feed on it and on no other plant, the gulf fritillary, (orange and black with three white spots on each wing) the variegated fritillary (orange and black) and the zebra longwing (black with pale yellow stripes). The zebra longwing is the Florida state butterfly. The caterpillars have worked things out so that they don't compete with each other. The zebra longwing (pale blue) only feeds on young end-shoots and likes the sun. The gulf and variegated fritillary (orange) feed on older leaves and prefers plants in the shade. They can eat the plant down to its roots, but what a display of butterflies when they hatch! A roosting of twenty to thirty adults together is a common sight. Bees and hummingbirds also like the nectar and mockingbirds eat the seeds.

The plant is tolerant of sandy, well-drained soils and is drought tolerant. It needs to be planted where it is protected from heavy winds and salt water intrusion. It can grow in full sun or light shade. They seed readily so pay attention to weeding wayward ones. They grow as much as three inches a day.

An example can be found on the south side of Flagler Avenue at 6th street on the chain link fence around a pocket park. A one-gallon plant can be purchased for $5.

Flowers

Giant Milkweed *(Calotropis gigantea)*

Creation Wins in Fearsome Lord Shiva's Favorite Flower.

"The gods would not refuse even the trivial *erukku* for worship," states the *Purananuru*, written 2000 years ago. The *erukku* is the not so trivial giant milkweed *(Calotropis gigantea.)* In India the fearsome god that they are referring to is the Lord Shiva, the Hindu god of destruction, the angry god, the god of darkness. But he is also the god of creation and his name means auspicious or welfare, implying that in every disaster there is also opportunity. Indian women gather the *Calotropsis* flowers and thread them onto strands, making garlands to drape over the pictures and statues of Shiva like giant lavender pearls.

Shiva has reproductive power which restores what has been destroyed. His symbol is the *lingam*, a stone representation of the phallus. These *lingams* are erected in Shiva's many temples across India and also under banyan trees in street-side shrines. They are kept covered with *Calotropis* garlands.

The *Calotropis* is considered of low status in the plant kingdom but it grows to a height of sixteen feet. In nature it occurs as scattered individuals. It is appropriate that this plant, which grows like a weed across Africa, Asia, Australia and the Caribbean, should be considered a favorite of the god of fertility.

The plant, also known as French cotton, crown flower or *bonba* in Spanish, is a soft wooded, evergreen shrub. Its long limbs hold six- to eight-inch opposite leaves that come from a clasping, heart-shaped base and end in a blunt point. They are celadon green, thick, leathery and covered with white fuzz that will rub off. The bark is corky and furrowed. When the stem or leaf is cut, copious amounts of white sap flows from the tip. Many people are allergic to this sap. The latex is toxic and can cause blisters and rashes on sensitive people. Eating this poisonous plant can cause the heartbeat to slow into hypotension and death.

The seeds form like our more familiar orange flowering milkweed plant and when pods break open, hundreds to thousands of seeds float like gossamer parachutes sending them flying like dandelions from each plant. In recent propagation, eighty-seven percent germinated in potting soil in as little as seven days. Its fecundity is legendary. In Key West it might be a good idea to cut the seed pods off before seeds fly away and create a serious weed problem. Growing quickly, it could easily become an exotic invasive, albeit a beautiful one. It is not on any invasive list–yet. *Calotropis* can also be easily propagated from cuttings. They do not grow well in the shade.

The *Calotropis* loves soils with high salt saturation, lives on beachfront dunes, is drought tolerant, can take the salt spray from the ocean and loves the bright sun.

Giant milkweed has almost no surface lateral roots, but it has a tap root that can grow nine feet into the ground. If it is cut back to the ground it will re-grow, making it almost hurricane proof.

The root bark is used to treat a variety of illnesses: leprosy, fever, malaria and snake bite. Sheep, goats and camels will eat the leaves.

One reason to keep this exotic is its unique lavender flowers. They form in clusters on the tips of the branches. Each flower is a pearl in the garland made for the *lingum*. It is beautiful, flowering profusely year round. You can see this plant in the butterfly garden at the Key West Garden Club and purchase it at the fall garden sale.

The plant that I have was totally destroyed by the larval stage of the monarch butterfly. I noticed hundreds of yellow eggs on the leaves and a while later the unique stripes of the many caterpillars that covered the plant. Despite the plant being completely devoured, I cut it back and it grew new leaves and is now lovely again. Of course, Lord Shiva, perhaps blowing his conch horn and holding his trident, is calling the monarchs back from Mexico and his special giant milkweed is awaiting their fecundity.

Seaside Gentian, Marsh Gentian (*Eustoma exaltatum*)

Lavender Wildflowers Surprise the Gardener

I was taking a walk along the beach last spring and I spotted an unusual lavender flower on a tall pale green weed. The flower was an open cup with a deep yellow center surrounded by a darker purple ring. It had five petals and sat at the end of a three-foot long stalk. There was only one, standing in all its glory, and I cherished it because of its singularity. I went right upstairs and checked out its name in my wildflower book.

Its name, *Eustoma,* comes from the Greek and means open mouth or good mouth. The flower emerges rolled tightly into a ball and then opens its mouth under the sun to form an inch and a half cup with yellow pistils and stamen. In the evening, it rolls itself up again. The second half of the name *exaltatum* is Latin for lofty, referring to the upright height of its stem. Some botanists argue that it is *Lisianthus* not *Eustioma*. There are also many common names for this wildflower, such as seaside gentian, prairie gentian, bluebells and even Lizzies.

This spring, much to my delight, there are fifty of them spread along the edge of the beach path. I can only happily assume that this native of the Keys seeds itself with abandon and has selected this small section of the beach as its chosen home. Sometimes the flower is white, but it always has the dark purple center. Since 1983, nurseries have been hybridizing the plant and have created many varieties in many different colors.

The leaves are fleshy, gray-green and clasp the stem on opposite sides. They are two inches long and half as wide ending in a point. The stalks branch out to form multiple ends where a flower will bloom. When the wind blows, the stalks sway merrily, bobbing their purple heads. There will be flowers, buds and seed pods on the same plant at the same time.

The *IRC Natives for Your Neighborhood* website says that these flowers need constant water and grow in poorly drained areas. I surmise that the roots of my plants go down into the water table level because they are growing in the low side of the berm in the sand dunes near the beach. They certainly grow in well drained soil as it is simply nutrient-poor sand. They are in the full sun and take the salt wind well. They also can take an inundation of salt water as long as it doesn't stay there long. They are happy in a drought. These showy flowers grow wild in the plains states of the Dakotas, Nebraska, Kansas and Texas and were a favorite of Lady Bird Johnson.

The plants do not bunch but grow separately, a few inches apart from each other. They are annuals but obviously seed well. They are not tasty, so grazers generally leave them alone. I cut several off and put them in water and they lasted about a week. They bloom from December through August.

These would be best planted with other low ground covers. I suggest that they would be lovely popping out of a bed of ambrosia or low *Spartina* grass. Think of them growing amongst the grasses of the prairies, little blue bonnets cavorting with the plainer grasses.

They are very difficult to propagate from seed because the seeds are so tiny, but they proliferate in the ditches along Rest Beach, growing in the exhaust of the traffic next to them. Whatever their name, these wildflowers are a delightful surprise when they pop up in the wild.

Shrimp Plant (*Justici brandegeana, Pachysstachys lutea, & Blechum pyramidatum*)

Names of Plants Explain Their Botanical History

The colorful shrimp plant does not have the usual easy-care characteristics of a native because it is an exotic coming from the West Indies or Mexico. However, it is worth the extra trouble, as it blooms profusely year round and can brighten up the garden during months when few other flowers bloom.

Sometimes plants are named for what they look like. One common species of shrimp plant (*Justici brandegeana*) was named because the loose bracts look like the contours of a pink shrimp. Another, *Pachystachys lutea,* means thick spiked yellow and has a yellow bract and flower.

Other times they are named for botanists such as *Justici brandegeana* named after Scottish Botanist James Justice (1698-1763.) He is remembered for being the first to bring a pineapple to fruiting in Scotland. In the world of botany this is a big deal. The second name refers to Townsand Stith Brandagee (1843-1925) who, with his wife Mary Curren, wrote many California botany books. On their honeymoon they hiked from San Diego to San Francisco, botanizing all the way. This species can be colored various shades of dusky red.

A third type of shrimp plant is the green *Blechum pyramidatum.* Pliny the Elder used this Greek word which means fern-like, and the pyramid in the second name refers to the smaller shape of the green bracts and flowers. This plant is smaller than the other two and spreads through airborne seeds. All three varieties are in the Acanthaceae family.

Shrimps grow on thin stems and vary in height from one to three feet. They can spread if conditions are right. The white flowers droop and curl, held by bracts of red, yellow or green. Playfully, they stick out their tongues from between two lips. Children like to pull the flowers out and suck the nectar, depriving the butterflies and hummingbirds of their lunches similar to what we did with honeysuckle flowers in Nebraska. In the case of the green shrimp plant that means, they are depriving the beautiful green malachite and white peacock butterflies.

They will grow in part shade, alkaline soil, and have moderate salt tolerance. They seldom have pests, but if they do pick up something it is likely to be spider mites or scale. If your plant becomes leggy, consider planting a low ground cover underneath. Keeping the plant pruned also helps keep it full. Shrimps make great garden plants because they bloom almost continuously year round. If pruned at the tip, they become bushier and can become quite dense.

The three inch leaves are dark green, ovate (oval with a pointed tip on the end) and evergreen. The underside is downy. The yellow shrimps can grow to three feet, the red can grow to four feet and the green stay at about a foot in height. They can be planted in a pot and make excellent patio plants. Examples can be found at the Key West Garden Club in the Butterfly Garden.

These Mexican and West Indies natives can be propagated by seeds, cuttings or by division of clumps. The red shrimp plants root quickly in water. Shrimp plants are readily available for under $10 in nurseries.

Perfumed Spiderlily (*Hymenocallis latifolia*)

Shower Your Yard with Spectacular Spiderlily Flowers

After Hurricane Wilma, when the beach was washed clean of vegetation, one of the first plants to pop up was the resilient spiderlily. Poking their heads out of the sand dune were the leathery leaves of the rosette-shaped native, *Hymenocallis latifolia*. This lily is in the Amaryllis family and grows wild in Key West. The fat leaves help it survive salt water and its large underground tuber allows it to grow back to its three foot height even when the top leaves have been totally destroyed.

One would not expect that a survivor plant like the spiderlily would have such spectacular flowers, but in the summer the lily sends forth a stalk that comes from the center of the plant and extends beyond it, which has between ten and sixteen delicate white flowers. The flower begins with a slender tube five to six inches long which opens into a delicate membrane and six narrow five-inch petals that curve back, making the large flower look like it has spider legs. Large, oval seeds form at the end of the long flower stalk on the plant that can be as wide as five feet. It readily reseeds itself but is usually propagated by bulb divisions.

Hymen refers to the delicate membrane and *callis* refers to beauty. *Latifolia* means wide broad leaves. As beautiful as these flowers are, don't make the mistake of eating them or you may expire as they are poisonous. Luckily, no one drinks perfume as some species of the spider lily is

94

so fragrant that it is used in expensive Crabtree & Evelyn and Gucci perfumes. The blossoms I smelled around here were not particularly fragrant.

The spiderlily is an herbaceous perennial forb. I learned this lovely word in researching this plant. A forb is a plant that is not a grass but grows in a meadow, vascular, but without woody tissue. There's a word to throw around in casual, horticultural conversation. It comes from the Greek *phorbe* meaning to graze.

The plant grows on coastal beaches and thickets and grows quickly in sunlit Key West gardens. It is evergreen and therefore makes an impressive mass planting, an edging plant or a splendid specimen. Put it in a big patio pot and grow it like an amaryllis. Tolerant of drought, salt wind and salt water, this surprisingly adaptable plant can also thrive in moist soils.

Pollination occurs with insects that brush its stamens. I don't advise brushing them, as the pollen, like that of all lilies, is hard to remove and takes special care if you need to wash it out of clothes. The hawkmoth drinks the nectar, sporting a four-inch proboscis that coils in front of its mouth in order to reach the interior of the plant. This night-flying moth is occasionally mistaken for a hummingbird, as it is one of the few creatures capable of hovering in mid air. Much despised by tomato growers, the large, green caterpillar of this moth has a horn on its rear and, after it eats enough tomato leaves, becomes a hard jug-shaped capsule buried in the ground from which it emerges as a moth.

This is a Key West native and therefore has few diseases or pests. You can find examples at Ft. Zach between the divided entrance roads. These inexpensive plants are readily available in nurseries. Turn your yard into a xeriscaping showcase using these fragrant natives.

Walking Iris (*Neomarica longifolia*)

The Fecund Iris Creates New Plants by Walking

Marica is the name of a water nymph in the River Liris who often hides in the shade of a sacred Italian glen named for her. In this sacred grove, oracles revealed the future. Faunus, the Roman name for the better-known Greek god Pan, is a very old nature god. Together they produced Acis, a river god. The hooved Faunus was an aggressive lover of the nymphs, creating many children in his orgiastic pursuit of pleasure. Likewise the plant walking iris, *Neomarica longifolia,* is a prolific producer of babies.

This member of the Iridaceae family produces a small yellow flower that blooms for only one day, rests for a few days and then blooms again. It does this for four to six weeks. If you arrive at the right time in the early morning and touch the end of the unopened flower, it will pop into the perfectly-formed flower with three maroon spotted petals. It flowers year round. This flower would be an ideal choice for time-lapse photography. At the end of the day the flower will close and start preparing for its long stem (hence the *longiflolia,* long foliage*)* to drop to the ground where it will take root, thereby "walking."

As prolific as Faunus, the iris will spread over large areas. It has to be divided often. It is known among gardeners as the "gift iris" because it is passed along to friends. Grandma passes this plant down to her children and grandchildren.

The walking iris has long, one-inch wide leaves that emerge from the soil like long flat swords. It is said that there must be twelve of these narrow, evergreen leaves on the plant before

96

the yellow flower will rise from the center. Some know this plant as the apostle plant because twelve apostles surround the flower-child Jesus. However, I have planted these and gotten flowers with as few as eight leaves.

Neomaricas will grow in the shade, part sun or full sun. It can flower and reproduce anywhere. It likes to be damp and prefers soil that drains well. It is doing well in the salty Key West soil and air, but I do not know if it will survive a hurricane because it is not a native of Key West but of Brazil. It does survive winters up north and will come back in the spring so it might make it through a hurricane-induced flood if the saltwater doesn't stand too long.

John Belden Ker originally named the plant *Marica* but he made a mistake, as another plant had that name, and botanists had to rename it *Neo* (new) *marica*. It is also called toad cups. This plant has no pests.

There are fifteen species of *Neomarica,* ranging in color from white to blue with orange and yellow markings (*N. caeruela*) and white with blue edges (*N. gracilis).*

It can be planted in pots and grown on the patio. It actually likes to be pot bound. Be careful around pets, as every part of it is poisonous. It looks marvelous planted among ferns because its three-foot upright foliage and the bright flower poking out create a lush landscape.

The nymph Marica was able to change the shape of beings, turning them into reeds or trees or maybe even walking iris. Faunus may still be hiding in the hammocks, a Roman nature god among us. Certainly this prolific plant is proof that nature is still full of fecundity. You can see this plant at the Key West Garden Club.

GROUNDCOVERS

Ambrosia (*Ambrosia hispida*)

The Immortal Ambrosia Plant Is No Food for the Gods

During the Civil War thirty-five-year-old Francis Payre Porcher, MD, was dispatched by the Confederate Surgeon General to wander the southern landscapes and codify all the native plants that could be used as medicines in order to augment supplies that might get blockaded. (Key West played a great part in that blockade, and some experts say, even won the war for the North).

Ambrosia hispida shows up in the *Southern Fields and Forests, Medical Botany of the Confederate States*, published in 1863. It was used for fevers, as a substitute for quinine and, as it was bitter, was to be given with whiskey. Medicine was not always available, but alcohol was. It is now undergoing medical and pharmaceutical research analysis.

Its family, Asteraceae, is numerically the largest family in the flora of North America and is found from the polar deserts of the Arctic tundra to the scrub of the Sonoran Desert. It's in the same family as the sunflower.

This ground cover is a whispery, silvery green and adds unusual pale accents to a garden. Once established, it does not require watering. This warrior will stand up to salt winds and stay on duty during brief saltwater inundations. Four days of tropical storm Ike left its beach front branches unscathed. It doesn't need much to eat, but likes well-drained soil and lots of sun.

We seldom call it by its popular name, allowing the verbal delights of "ambrosia" to supersede the negative connotations of "beach ragweed." Ambrosia was the food of the Greek gods but its use in the naming of this plant is ironic. The name comes from the Greek word meaning immortal. This plant *is* immortal in the sense that in many parts of the world it is impossible to get rid of it. If you plant it you'll need to trim it often.

The yellowish-green male and whitish-green female flowers form terminal spikes on the same plant. Then small burrs form and the seeds can be transported by wildlife. Birds like to eat these seeds and it is a host plant for butterflies and moths. Electrostatically-charged honey bees accumulate pollen as they collect nectar and it is frequently found as a component of raw honey.

It flowers all year long, a negative for allergy-prone individuals. It is found in open coastal areas, but is rather rare. Interestingly, the pollen, which is spread by the breeze, does not spread if the humidity is over 70%. Here in Key West, the pollen clumps up and rarely blows away. That may be the reason that the plant is not found frequently in the wild in coastal areas.

Use this plant in your garden to create texture and offset darker greens or on your patio or balcony. As a container plant it cascades over the edges of the pot and forms falling vines. It spreads quickly on the ground through rooting rhizomes on its stems and can be easily clipped and propagated in that way. It has no serious diseases or pests.

The Key West Garden Club has an excellent specimen in the Native Plant area which survived the ire of the gods in the winds of tropical storm Ike quite splendidly.

Debbie Crowley propagating ambrosia

Bromeliads *(Aechmea blanchetiana)*

Randy Bromeliads Make Showy Garden Guests

Key West Garden Club bromeliad enthusiast Jackie Thomas was introduced at the club's monthly meeting as having a green thumb she inherited from her mother, Lois Kitching, who was a bromeliad expert. "But my mother always said that she had a black thumb," Thomas quipped to her overflowing audience, "because it takes manure to get a plant to grow here."

Bromeliads are native to the Americas, from the southern part of the U.S. to the middle of Argentina. The Bromelioideae family was named by Charles Flomier after Olaf Bromel.

Their sharp leaves and water-filled whorls were bizarre enough to impress Christopher Columbus, who took samples back to Europe on his second voyage to the New World in 1493. By 1776, bromeliads had become a sensation in Europe, spawning a new fad for wealthy botanists who built personal greenhouses to house and propagate the exotic bromeliads. Luckily these plants propagate easily.

"Bromeliads are so randy that pups will always be popping up," Thomas said. "This is a very promiscuous plant."

By 1828, growers had begun hybridizing the bromeliads and now there are over 100,000 varieties. Bromeliads grow from sea level to 6,000 feet. They grow in tropical climates and in deserts. Although most of them are from the Americas, they are also found on the hump of Africa that broke off from the South American continent some 66 million years ago. Some of them need soil; others grow in the air, subsisting on dew and rain.

The most popular bromeliads fall into four categories: the pineapple, which is native to the Caribbean, not Hawaii; the *Guzmania lingulata* with its gorgeous red and yellow inflorescence; the *Aechmea fasciata*, a pink urn type whose inflorescence lasts for months; and the *Vriesea splendens*, which can be found at stores like Kmart.

A few days before the lecture at the Garden Club meeting, Thomas provided a hands-on propagation workshop where she attached a large *Aechmea blanchetiana* to a *Lignum vitae* tree. (This bromeliad retails for around $60). After removing the pup, she cleaned out the interior pocket of debris and then further cleaned it by dipping it in a weak solution of bleach and water. Pulling off stubborn dead or damaged lower leaves was made easier by her trick of slitting the leaf length-wise before attempting to remove it.

"These leaves are serrated and sharp. When I handle them I wear welding gloves that go up to my upper arm," Thomas warned.

There were terrestrial roots on the bromeliad so, since she was mounting it in a tree instead of planting it in the ground, she cut off all of the roots and dipped the remaining stem in a root enzyme.

"Choose a tree with a low fork for best viewing and rough bark for best adherence," she said. "The stem needs to fit closely in the fork. New roots that grow will eventually hold the plant on the tree, but they are thin and will break in a breeze if the bromeliad is not firmly stabilized, so tie or strap the bromeliad firmly." Thomas then used Liquid Nails to glue the plant to the tree. (This does not hurt the tree in any way).

"Once established, the bark will pull off the tree before the roots will loosen," Thomas said. She suggested putting Spanish or sphagnum moss around the root area to retain moisture. Finally, she trimmed the damaged leaves, shaping them like the other leaves.

The bromeliad has two sources of food: first the nutrients it absorbs from the water that collects in the cup in the center of the plant and second, from the nutrients it gets from the earth. Not all bromeliads need the earth. Many can be planted in trees and will thrive as air plants. They also are spectacular as potted plants. Try placing a pair of them at an entryway.

Fertilize the bromeliad with a weak solution and it will grow prodigiously. Red bracts with showy yellow flowers will delight the owner in the spring. It is drought tolerant, but not particularly salt tolerant. It has few pests, but give it too much water and it is prone to root rot. Butterflies, birds and bees love it, especially hummingbirds.

Burn Jelly Plant *(Bulbine frutescens)*

Bulbine Is South Africa's Contribution to Xeriscaping

Bulbine is a ground cover, similar to aloe vera in its medicinal properties because it contains the same glycoprotein. Its jelly-like juice is used to treat burns, rashes, blisters, insect bites, ringworm, cracked lips, acne, cold sores, and a kid's knocks and scrapes, although it may stain the skin brown. Claims are made that it will cure leprosy, skin cancer and allergies. Rastafarians make a tea from its leaves that they use for colds and arthritis. It is also used to reduce scar tissue.

It loves the alkaline soil common to Key West and is water-wise, growing in near desert conditions. Poor soil is helpful to its growth as long as the soil is well drained...like ours. It blooms year round in the bright sun.

This plant should be a native xeriscaping plant, but it is not. It is from South Africa. I checked the Category I, II and III exotic invasive list and it was not listed. Being perfectly acclimated to the conditions in the Keys, it should do well here. I'm sure it loves growing in Key West as much as all the northern transplants, who decide to move here after one winter vacation.

This succulent has narrow, six- to eight-inch long leaves that are fleshy and light green. They look like scallions. The orange flowers surround fluffy yellow stamens and are small, six-petaled and star-shaped. They are set on a tall raceme or stalk that rises above the leaves. Blooms last a long time but when they are finished should be dead-headed for best re-blooming results. It grows fast and forms clumps with its rhizomatous roots spreading outward.

Bulbine comes from the Asphodelaceae family with more than fifty species. It has previously been classified in the Liliaceae family by botanists, but, despite its being named *Bulbine*, which means onion or bulb, it does not actually have a bulbous base. Carl Ludwing von Wildenow is credited with finding this plant. One common cultivar, Hallmark, is named after famed African botanist, Harry Hall, and has sterile seeds.

It is used in rock gardens and as a ground cover in drought resistant places where it is difficult to plant. Small black seeds will also spread via wind if it is not a sterile species. Growing quickly, it can fill up a container in a few months so it is an excellent patio plant. Be careful that you do not over water A light freeze may kill the leaves, but it will often grow back. It needs dividing frequently and can be easily propagated with the divided cuttings. Give it plenty of room to spread.

I do not know how it reacts to salt water, but it seems to take the salt wind well. It has no diseases or pests. Bees and butterflies love its nectar and deer and rabbits also are fond of the leaves. You can see it growing at the Key West Garden Club on the top of the hill.

Caladium (*Caladium ssp.*)

Amazon Natives Play Well in Key West Yards

Within earshot of the "Beat, beat, beat of the tom-tom," along the shady Amazon River basin, grows the colorful caladium. It also grows well in our well-drained, warm soil and our humid summer environment. We don't even have to dig these tubers up during their dormant dry winter months as they do up north. They are perfectly happy to sleep until April and pop up again as a springtime surprise.

Gardeners love these shady fellows as they add a splash of color to lightless areas in which flowers are difficult to grow. Like the song, their heart-shaped leaves declare "It's love, it's love, it's love" in green, purple, pink, red and white. Varieties, like our love lives, are endless. These shady creatures have names to match their unique natures: Freida Hemple and Postman Joyner could share a bed, as could Fire Chief and June Bride or Brandywine and White Christmas. Couples with more sunny natures, Rosebud and Red Flash could unite in a colorful red bed.

If you are going to plant new ones, spring is the time. Think of the tuber like a potato, not a bulb. It has a bumpy eye on top that will grow leaves and a flat lower part that will grow the roots. If you mix them up, don't worry, the leaves will find their way to the top and the roots to the bottom. However it will be a little stockier if it has to do the flip underground.

Plant them 1½ to 2 inches underground, water well and wait patiently. They may take as long as two months before they begin to grow, but when they do, they grow quickly. Nights must be at or above 75 degrees. Leaves will droop if they are thirsty as they are not drought tolerant. To promote leaf growth, remove the largest bud in the center of the tuber. The height of the caladium will be from twelve inches to three feet tall depending on the size of the original tuber. Small (1 ½ inch) tubers are $12 for twenty-five. Jumbo size ones are $45 for twenty-five tubers.

There is some controversy about fertilizing. Generally, use one teaspoon of a 6-6-6 every six weeks or a slow release style. However, if the plant gets too much fertilizer some of them turn all green and lose their unusual color, especially the white ones. Don't remove the center eye of the white ones, either, as they will turn all green.

Caladiums are in the Arum family. They have a fleshy stem with a fadex surrounded by a hood-like white flower, much like the peace lily. Other aroids are *Dieffenbachias*, *Anthuriums* and *Monstera deliciosa*. They are toxic if eaten, producing burning and swelling of the lips, nausea, vomiting and diarrhea. Some people also have minor skin reactions when handling the leaves. Wear gloves and don't eat them. Don't let your children, cats or dogs eat them, either.

Although caladiums originate in Brazil, Lake Placid, in south-central Florida, calls itself the Caladium Capital of the World. One thousand two hundred acres of land is planted in caladiums. Go to their 19th Annual Caladium Festival on August 28, 29, 30 to view the acres that have been planted by fourteen farmer families since the 1940's. They compare the experience to viewing the tulip fields of Holland.

Caladiums have no pests so there is no insecticide used on this land. Caladiums are great borders and circlets around trees. Plant them in shady areas next to the house or sprinkle in and around other vegetation. They create color under other vegetation at the Garden Club. Fine examples that the Trophia Butterfly Foundation just planted around the trunks of the giant gumbo limbo trees can be seen at the Little Truman White House restoration project. Caladiums are also great container plants for the patio or in window boxes.

All the gardener has to do is provide a bed for them and wait for them to multiply.

Golden Creeper (*Emodea littoralis*)

Frolicking Groundcovers Native to the Kooky Keys

When I think of the glorious golden creeper (*Ernodea littoralis*), I always see children frolicking on the beach because the word *Ernodea* means like a young sprout and *littoralis* means on the beach. The narrow, one-inch long, succulent leaves of this plant, borne on bright red stems, are a fresh yellow-green. The square woody stems shoot out fine textured leaves that bob and dance in the ocean breezes. It has tiny white flowers with curled lobes that turn pink as they age. The flowers look like they were made for a baby girl. Although this plant looks delicate, it's as tough as any tomboy on the beach. That Rubiaceae family sure can have fun.

This Keys native can grow to three feet high and two feet wide. It covers large sun drenched areas by moving along as the stems touch the ground and take root. Gardener Mom and Dad will marvel as it grows bigger and broader every week. Their baby creeps like crazy.

The State of Florida recommends that it be planted more frequently. It grows well in our nutrient-poor, well-drained soil. It behaves like a perfect child. Mommy and Daddy don't need to worry about a drought, salt winds or salty soil. It can take a brief flood and bounce right back. It's a perfect plant for those day-long hurricane inundations.

Why is it called the golden creeper? It flowers periodically throughout the year, after which it pops out clusters of small, round, golden berries shaped like tiny pomegranates but tasting like apples. The birds love the berries so the dancing children will have birds perched on their out-

106

stretched arms as they pick off golden berries. They'll be tickled as the birds flit through foliage. Small mammals like its berries.

It is also called wild pomegranate, *ernodia de playa* and cough bush. A tea made from its leafy branches can be used as a home made remedy for coughs.

This flirty plant has outstanding ornamental value as it adds an airy, light hue and fine texture to a sunny garden. It will thrive in a sunny area on the south side next to a sidewalk or road. It holds sand together and will grow right on a beach or in a rock garden. It would look great between large, smooth bromeliads which also don't need watering.

There are no worries about insect pests or root rot problems as long as you allow it to stay dry. After it is established, don't water it at all. This plant is xeriscaping heaven. I priced Golden Creeper in a Homestead nursery at $3.25 for a one-gallon size and $8.50 for a seven gallon size.

Plant it outside your door so the dancing beach kids wave good-bye whenever you leave the house.

Sea Purslane *(Sesuvium portulacastrum)*

Pull it up. Chop it up. Serve It for Supper
Sea Purslane Is Nature's Edible Bounty

Sea purslane, *(Sesuvium portalacastrum),* can be found lurking along the curb, between cracks in the sidewalk, on rocky highway median strips and often as an unasked for intruder, a weed in Key West gardens. Pity the poor purslane, cursed with *tiny* pink or yellow flowers, as it gets yanked from the ground as a nuisance and reconsider its fate.

Purslane has been widely cultivated as food and has been used in salads for the last 2,000 years. Pull it up. Chop it up. Serve it for supper. It can be cooked with a little garlic and onion and makes a tasty side dish full of protein, omega 3 and vitamins A, B1, C and iron. Make an omelet with this herb or use its mucilage as a thickener for soups. This lowly weed has saved people from famine.

At organic food markets, I find big bunches priced at around three dollars. The variety that grows along the Atlantic Ocean is too salty to eat, but the plants that grow a bit inland have the crisp, fresh taste of succulents. Its seeds are edible raw or cooked and are used in bread making. Use it like spinach, although it is a better nutrient source than spinach. Wild purslane is tastier than the cultivated varieties. Turtles find it tasty, as do birds, rabbits and deer.

You can recognize the groundcover by its reddish stems and its juicy, fat succulent leaves. Both the stems and leaves are edible. The stems can be a little tough but the leaves are soft, green on the top and pale rose on the bottom. It grows tight to the ground when there is little rain, but can rise to its full height of eight inches with water.

The flowers come from the end of the stems and open in the bright sun. On cloudy days or in the evening, leaves and flowers close up. This herb flowers all year long, grows in nutrient poor soil, tolerates salt wind and even floods. It's often the first plant to show up on the beach after a hurricane, stabilizing the sand. It spreads quickly to form broad patches. The name *Sesuviium* refers to a Gallic tribe mentioned by Caesar. I bet they ate it.

Maybe sea purslane won't make your weed tolerance list, but there are commercial varieties available at inexpensive prices that have much bigger flowers. Commonly known as moss roses, *(Portulaca grandiflora),* they have dazzling, inch-long, jewel-tone flowers with colors that range from yellow, peach, fuchsia, orange, white, and pink to purple. The flat, wild, rose-like flowers look like confetti flung across the sunny planting bed. Although they are annuals, they self seed. If you don't want the plant to spread, pick the seed pods off, as a single plant can produce 50,000 seeds.

Portulaca means to carry milk for the sappy white substance in its stems. *Grandiflor* means great flower.

Both MARC House and Home Depot sell them inexpensively and you can tell what color you are getting. The seeds are tiny, so mix them with sand before you sow them. They germinate within two weeks. The plant can also be propagated by cuttings. Put the cuttings in water and wait a week. Some people report simply sticking the cutting in the ground.

This is a great ground cover, but you can't walk on it as it breaks the soft stems. It would be good in a rock garden or between stepping stones or along the driveway. It also can be grown as a hanging plant on a balcony. If you want more flowers, pinch the dead-heads off. It loves heat, sun and drought. If they overrun the sidewalk or drive, pruning the plants is no problem. They grow back thicker.

If aphids are a problem, spray water on the plant. Mealy bugs only occasionally bother it. If it gets white pustules, it has white rust, and those infected parts should be cut off. Root rot can be a problem if you water it too much. That is not likely to happen in our well drained soils, but over-zealous pot-gardeners should beware of heavy hands on the watering can.

Next time you find sea purslane cluttering up your yard, remember, it can be lunch.

GARDEN CLUB LECTURES

Photos of the Garden Club after Hurricane Wilma by Rosi and Jeff Ware

Welcome the Rains That Come after Storms or Hurricanes

Tropical storms can pour saltwater and blow salt winds over our gardens for days at a time. They can be equally as damaging as hurricane force winds. Afterwards, plants need special care and speed may be very important.

First, survey the yard for major damage. Trees that have been knocked over need to be righted as soon as possible and staked with three stakes. Make sure the stakes are outside the root area. Use soft material such as canvas or strong cloth to secure the trunk to the stakes. These stakes can stay in for the next year while the tree re-establishes its fine root system, but remember to check their fit as the tree is growing.

As soon as possible after the storm passes, trees should be sprayed with a strong stream of water to remove the salt from their leaves. If you have salty silt around the roots, wash it away as the roots need air to survive, but not too much air. Soil can be loosened when a tree is blown this way and that. Check to make sure that there are no air pockets that will dry the roots out. Watering the plant every two days will wash the soil into small air pockets and wash the salt out of the soil. Replace any missing soil, but do not cover up the trunk.

If the tree is too large for a homeowner to stand up, cover the roots with debris, downed leaves, or moist towels, anything to keep the roots from being exposed to the drying air. Even trunks and limbs can get sunburned if exposed to direct sun. Call an arborist to right the tree. This may take heavy equipment. It is possible that the tree will die immediately, or the damage may not show up for several years. Do not add fertilizer as it could burn the newly forming fine roots. Do mulch out to the edge of the limb line, but keep the mulch a foot away from the trunk of the tree.

If the tree is upright but has broken some branches, cut the branches back to just after their entrance to the main trunk. It is important to do this as disease and insects can damage raw broken branches more easily than ones that have clean cuts. Use a saw and make a sharp even cut. No painting of the wound is necessary. If the branches are large or too high up in the tree, call an arborist who knows how to handle larger problems. The arborist also might advise you to remove some of the leaves and branches to reduce water demand or advise you to cut other healthy branches to create a more even tree and prevent further storm damage.

Water everything well to remove the salt. Bushes and groundcovers should be sprayed to minimize salt wind damage. Do not wait to see the damage before you act. It will be too late. A good hard rain after a salt spray is excellent for the leaves. Don't be in a rush to cut down good trees that have lost their leaves. The leaves on native trees will come back in time.

Less damage occurs if the plantings are native. Our local flora has withstood hurricanes for centuries. If you have lost an exotic plant, think about replacing it with a native that will survive Key West weather.

Kim Gabel from the University of Florida Agricultural Extension in Monroe County has listed some important lessons learned in the 2005 hurricane season. I want to share some of them with you. Proper care of your landscape will result in less storm damage.

1. Plant natives, especially Spanish stopper, gumbo limbo, lignum vitae, joewood, seven year apple, white stopper, sea grape, bay cedar, buttonwoods, Jamaica caper, spider lilies, native grasses, cabbage palms and thatch palms. (Check the web site at www.regionalconservation.org for detailed descriptions of native plants at IRC Natives for Your Neighborhood.)
2. Call your local arborist to prune your trees to get rid of bark inclusions, co-dominant trunks, and thick leaf crowns. This strengthens the tree.
3. Keep the tree roots healthy.
4. Wash and water the affected plants. Water frequently to cleanse the soil.

Rosi Ware, President Emeritus, whacks away.

Spring Is the Season to Whack Them Down to Size

Do not be intimidated by your plants. Spring is the season to chop them off, in a most delicate manner, but still, whack them down to the right size. "When Northerners newly transplanted to the Keys go about pruning their plants they often start with a paltry six inches off the branch. They soon learn that the rate of growth in this warm, humid climate can put six inches on a plant in a week," said Rosi Ware, president-emeritus of the Key West Garden Club. A passel of Garden Club volunteers were attacking the overgrown *Jatropha*, *Cassia*, golden dewdrop, jasmine, *Heliconia*, beautyberry and many other plants last week when I stopped by on their Monday volunteer work day.

Rosi pulled branch after branch out of an overgrown corner of the garden, "It's time to prune before the summer rains come. The gardens get overgrown through the winter."

Plants may have been damaged by insects or diseases and those branches should come off. They may need to conform to a specific shape, not spill over the sidewalk or driveway or overhang a path. Your plants will not be angry with you for taking the clippers to them, but will reward you with vigorous growth and prodigious flowering.

First, let's talk about tools. They need to be kept well-oiled and sharp. Your plants will not like being gnawed at by blunt instruments. There are two varieties of hand pruners, the snap-cut variety used for larger cuts and the scissors type, which cost more, but produce smoother cuts. Lopping shears, which have long handles, will give you better leverage. Finally, there are hedge shears which have very long blades. Cherish your tools and clean them with alcohol after each use so you don't spread diseases among plants.

Moving into the tools for larger jobs, you might need one of the many varieties of saws or even a combination pole-saw pruner for taller branches. Do not attempt to prune major tree branches; you will need an arborist for that.

Now that you are armed, your next problem is where to cut. The plant produces a hormone called auxin in its terminal bud. That's the one on the end. This hormone directs the growth of the buds on the sides of the branch. When you cut the terminal bud off, the lateral ones begin growing. Most of the growth will occur within six to eight inches of the cut.

Carefully look at the branch to decide at what height you want to begin the new growth. Then look for a node, a lateral branch or the main trunk and cut *very* close to that point. That area has most of the plant's healing hormone and therefore the cut will heal quickly. If you leave too much stub, the plant has a harder time healing and the branch may become diseased or die back.

Avoid using electric shears to whack off the top of the plants. Shearing leaves and branches with electric clippers produces leggy plants with leaves on the exterior only. It is better to thin the plant first, because it will bring more light into the interior leaves and second, because it gives your plant a more graceful look. If you are working on a hedge, make sure that the bottom of the hedge is slightly wider than the top so that light can get to all of the leaves.

Often in this column I have talked about a plant as either a tree or a shrub. Often you can determine which you want your plant to be and how many trunks you want it to have by pruning. I recently pruned off all of the low branches of a firebush in order to make it a twelve foot tree with a canopy of red flowers and a single stem. There is an amazing golden dewdrop topiary in Southeast Asia that is sixty feet tall and consists of a series of two foot balls separated by two feet of trunk, so making a tree out of one is an easy task with a little patience.

If you have planted a shrub that has gotten quite out of hand over the years, you may want to cut it back to the ground leaving just eight inches of trunk and let it start all over again. Coral bean, bougainvillea and beautyberry respond well to this type of cutting. The second growth will be fast as the plant already has a substantial root system to support the growth. After hurricanes, when the foliage has been extensively damaged, this renewal pruning works very well.

Cut off root suckers, low growing branches that interfere with foot traffic, water sprouts (upright growing branches) and branches that rub against other branches as well as branches that compete with the leader for dominance. These shoots starve the plant of nutrients. Cut those suckers off.

Don't be afraid to prune even young plants. They will behave better as they grow older and you won't have a difficult teenager later. Discipline! Courage! You can rear a great plant!

Mary Sandusky

Eloise Pratt

Caro Le-fort

Kitty Somerville, Director of Propagation, displaying the air-layered orchid tree branch.

Air Layering a Sterile Orchid Tree

"We think of this as a science project," said Kitty Somerville, plant propagator at the Key West Garden Club. "We were excited to try something new." Last May, at the beginning of the rainy season Kitty and her compatriots at the Key West Garden Club--Sue Sullivan and Mary Sandusky--got a lesson on air rooting from Pat Rogers, a Garden Club member and professional horticulturalist. She chose a tree in the West Martello Garden Club grounds--the Hong Kong orchid tree *(Bauhinia x blakeana)*.

This plant produces no seeds, therefore is great for Key West because it is not invasive like other orchid trees, but it also presents a problem. If you want another one of these gorgeous thirty-foot, flowering trees, you must embark upon the somewhat scary mutilation of a branch of the original. You may be heartened by the fact that the tree needs pruning to make it less brittle and to produce a rounded crown, so wounding it is actually doing the tree a favor.

"We had to learn not to be afraid to cut the bark away," Kitty said. "Pat guided us through the process." She started by asking Garden Club members to do several practice cuts on some smaller expendable branches of a variegated gardenia with red flowers. They used a razor sharp blade to make the incisions that would strip off about three inches of the bark and cadmium layer without damaging the rest of the branch. They circled around the branch and then made a straight incision from the top circle to the bottom one and peeled off the bark.

After Kitty and Sue carefully cut around the branch, they took sphagnum moss that they had soaked overnight in water, squeezed it out and wrapped it thickly around the wound using string to keep the moss in place. Keeping the area wet so that the new roots grow is essential, so they wrapped the moss in clear plastic wrap, taping it closed on the ends with electrical tape right on the tree bark so that no moisture escaped. That wasn't enough. They then wrapped the entire plastic in aluminum foil. Why? Roots like to be kept in the dark. After poking small holes in the plastic wrap, they watered weekly.

Finally, they got to the orchid tree. Pat chose a branch about one inch wide that would not take away from the tree's shape. After three months, they were rewarded with great looking roots that could be seen through the plastic. Just to make sure the tree would have enough roots to survive planting, they waited another three months.

When the cuttings were ready, Pat used a sharp knife to cut the branches about two inches below the moss balls, took off the aluminum foil and plastic and potted them, being careful not to disturb the root ball. Key West has such high humidity that it was not necessary to acclimatize the cutting by putting a plastic bag over it. In a few weeks, they could see the cutting had established itself as a independent plant.

"We couldn't believe it worked so well!" Kitty said. "It took time, but it was worth it."

A valuable web site, "Air Layering for Difficult-to-Root Plants" by Everett E. Janne of Texas A & M University has clear illustrations and instructions on this process. (http://aggie-horticulture.tamu.edu/extension/ornamentals/airlayer/airlayer.html) If you want to try this method of propagating, check out the pictures to see how terrific the plant will look when it is potted.

Jacki Pessolano of Keys Florist and Gifts

Flower Arranging at the Garden Club

"I like the bizarre," began Jackie as she spoke to the Key West Garden Club at their April Meeting. "My flower arrangements are influenced by the mood that I am in when I design them. Of course, I also listen to the sentiment preferred by the recipient." Thus began a lesson in how to turn weird flowers into vibrant arrangements from Jackie Pessolano of Keys Florist and Gifts on Cudjoe Key who has been arranging for twenty-five years.

"It's like art," Jackie said, "it's all in the eye of the beholder," and from there she began with the mechanics of arranging. First choose the vase. Soak green Oasis foam in a bucket of water before you put it into the vase. Tape the foam securely into the vase and add more water. (Tape and foam are available at most grocery and hobby stores.) Usually, the height of the arrangement is two and a half times the width.

You might see Jackie's construction on a local hotel reception desk. First, she added greens to hide the mechanics. She used unusual greens, but you might use backyard ferns or branches with small leaves and seeds. The seeds add texture to the lower level. A quick whisk with some spray-on vegetable oil gave the leaves sheen. Next, she marked a center point, the tallest section of the display using three orange bird of paradise flowers, spreading the ones that were still closed with her fingers.

For color variation she popped in three pink and green baby pineapple stems. Locals might try using interesting sticks, aloe flowers or woman's tongue, an exotic invasive plant. She built the background with more leather leaf, added two protea, (fuzzy, three-inch round, yellow balls) red coffee beans and a few yellow billy balls. She bent large dark leaves, connecting their stems with their leaf tips. Then she stapled them together (Yes, with a stapler!) and put them in on one side of the arrangement. Lastly, she checked to make sure that there was enough interest in the back. This arrangement took half an hour.

The second arrangement was a rose nosegay. This could be done with local flowers such as blanket flower, *Ixora* or ground orchids. Strip the leaves from the flowers. After the flowers are arranged in a tight circle, secure rubber bands around the stems at the top and bottom. Always trim flower stems at a slant. Add small green leaves at the bottom of the chosen vase to disguise the trimmed stems. Hide the rubber bands with ribbons. This easy powder room or bedroom bouquet took Jackie thirteen minutes.

The last arrangement was in a round, clear glass bowl. On top of the bowl she crisscrossed tape. Inside the bowl was a strand of grape vine. Then she popped three large sunflowers with very short stems into the vase and added some greens to cover the top edges. Voila! There was a five-minute, low bouquet suitable for a dinner party.

Jackie can produce monumental arrangements with a unique flair for special occasions, but we can all arrange using her key elements. Don't be afraid to choose unusual flowers, seeds, berries and leaves. Secure your mechanics. Start with a focal point. Let your eye, your emotions and the nature of the plant material be your guide.

Check out the monthly-changing floral arrangements at the Key West Garden Club.

Nan Lindas and Roberta Lowe instruct the Garden Club how to make living wreaths

Wreath Making at the Key West Garden Club

"How to Make a Living Holiday Wreath" was the subject of the December Garden Club lecture. Nan Lindas from MARC Plant Store and MARC volunteer Roberta Lowe created a cornucopia of holiday decorations while demonstrating how to create luscious wreaths. The advantage of a living wreath is that it does not dry out and have to be discarded and therefore can hang year round.

They started out with pre-made wreath bases made from grape vines. These are ideal as they create a surface into which it is easy to tie wire. Ann Eid suggested that the aerial roots of the strangler fig might be a good substitute as grape vines are unknown around town. The roots must be soaked in water to make them pliable. After they are pliable they are wrapped in a circle and held together with wire as they dry.

Beginning with the vine base, Nan and Roberta created the living part of the wreath composed of Spanish moss wrapped around the grape vines where they wanted to create the living sculpture. Nan wrapped approximately half of a fourteen inch wreath with the moss. Since the wreaths have no water, the living section of the wreath consists of air plants *(Tillandsias)* and seed pods, thistles, pine cones, dried mushrooms and dried seeds. Walk around your garden or keep your eye out for native components. One of the cones that they used was from our local Australian pine. These items are tied on the wreath with florist wire. If this is difficult, try using a crochet hook to pull the wire through the vines. Even the seed pods are fastened with wire as the glue from a glue gun will not hold after exposure to our high humidity, sun and salt air.

Don't be afraid to extend the *Tillandsias* over the edge of the wreath and expand the boundary lines asymmetrically. Living wreaths do not require bows as they are often meant to be left outside, however bows do add a holiday feeling. *Tillandsias* are available inexpensively.

Nan and Roberta also made fragrant fir wreaths. Again they began with pre-made fir wreaths. They fluffed them out so that the wreaths had depth and began tying on the ornaments.

Nan started with a double red bow tied to the top of the wreath. Some people consider themselves bow-challenged. Don't worry about how the bow looks until it is tied in the middle, then use the wire edges of the ribbon to straighten the bow. Do one large bow, tie it with wire, make a smaller bow and tie it to the larger one before you attach it to the wreath.

Nan chose a male and female cardinal and tiny nest with eggs to decorate her wreath. A small red ribbon was wound through the fir to tie the separate pieces together with color. Pine cones were wrapped with wire and placed in appropriate places on the branches. Roberta stuck in long cinnamon sticks and long sticks of dark brown wood, curled at the top, for a more natural look.

Virginia Probert & Helen Koger

Patti Rodriguez

Gail Knapp, Karen Contraras, Patti Rodriguez, Mary Sandusky, Margret Nygren, Debbie Crowley & Kitty Somerville

Karen Contreras and Mary Sandusky

Hunt for Native Orchid Requires a Walk on the Wild Side

By Kitty Somerville

"The orchids in Watson Hammock are starting to bloom!" read the email from Kim Gabel, Monroe County Extension Office. It was music to my ears and I immediately signed up for the guided field trip, exclusive to Master Gardeners and limited to twelve participants.

The thrill of hiking to find an orchid, native to our area, brought back memories of reading the popular book, "The Orchid Thief." Was I crazy to plan to hike in a mosquito infested, soggy hammock?

We began our trip at the Blue Hole on Big Pine Key (MM 31), and, swimming in it, for our enjoyment, was an alligator. Our guide, Ben Edwards, with the Big Pine Wildlife Rescue, explained that the Blue Hole was an abandoned limestone quarry. It has a layer of freshwater over salt water and the fresh water attracts the alligators. "OK," I thought. "I can do this because we will not be in fresh waters to see the orchid."

A fellow Master Gardener, Nancy MacKenzie, lives on Big Pine Key and hikes in the Hammock with Edwards. Two months ago they saw the orchids start their flower spike and two weeks ago they saw some bloom.

As Edwards began the hike, he casually mentioned that the three most common snakes in the area are black racers, corn and the diamondback rattler. Then he distracted us by pointing out a native locustberry *(Brysonima lucida)* that was in fruit. "You can eat the ripe fruit," Edwards indicated, and some of the brave hikers chowed down on the small red berry. No one grasped for

120

their throats, so we continued.

Watson Hammock, a tropical hardwood hammock, is a part of the National Key Deer Refuge. The refuge, established in 1957, is 9,200 acres, with critical habitat for federally listed species, such as the Key Deer. Although we were in an area that required a permit for the hike, there are trails open for the public. The Refuge visitor Center can be reached at (305) 872-0774.

Edwards is clearly enamored by the area and pointed out native wildflowers. Seaside gentian stood tall with a purple flower. Saltmarsh false foxglove had pink flowers and it is the larval host of the common buckeye butterfly. Then we saw the slender twining vine of the sky blue clustervine, which Edwards says was not in this area before Hurricane Wilma in 2005. There were beautiful air plants *(Bromeliads* and *Tillandsia)* scattered among the tree branches. The water was six feet high from the floods of Wilma and the only air plants that lived were above the water.

Cord grass, with needle-like stems, was stinging the hikers wearing shorts. We proceeded into the buttonwoods and mangroves and I was grateful that MacKenzie was in front of me to break the spider webs. Then part of a web went into my mouth. That was soon forgotten as the mosquitoes became thick. More than a dozen of the pesky insects were sitting on Edwards's hat. We soon found that they are attracted to black clothing, and Kim Gabel had a swarm following her. At times the brackish water was above our ankles.

Right ahead was the *Encyclia tampensis*, wrapped gently around a buttonwood. There were several plants in a ten foot area. This dainty protected orchid is commonly called a butterfly orchid and grows in U.S. Agricultural zones 9-11. Several flowers grace the spikes, each one to two inches across. They have green tepals streaked with brown and a white lip that has a rose-purple spot.

Encyclia tampensis was discovered by John Torrey in 1846 near Tampa, Florida. Its name *Encyclia* means to encircle and *tampensis* for the area of first discovery, Tampa.

The group stayed, along with the mosquitoes, taking pictures of the orchids, appreciating the moment and feeling the passion of the hunt. On the hike back, Edie Kehoe, Master Gardener, told me that she grew up in this area and played as a child in the hammock. She remembers the *Bromeliads,* thick in the trees, with memories of them being sold at the flea market. We are fortunate to have this protected area, so future gardeners with the same passion as we have, will be able to enjoy it in the future.

Kitty Somerville is a Master Gardener and 1st VP of the Key West Garden Club.

Photos by Kitty Somerville

121

"These gumbo limbo trees were propagated from branch cuts, because they have co-dominant trunks instead of one dominant trunk," explained Cynthia Domenech-Coogle, the City of Key West's urban forestry program manager.

McCoy Indigenous Park - A Local Treasure

By Cynthia Edwards

Bocce ball courts, birthday parties and birds are the face of McCoy Indigenous Park on White Street. Behind all that lies a truly local treasure, one of the few large plots of undeveloped natural land left in Key West. As the name indicates, most of the plants in the six acres are native (indigenous) to the Florida Keys; they consist mostly of hardwood hammock species, as City Urban Forestry Program Manager Cynthia Domenech-Coogle explained on a recent tour of the park.

Indigenous Park is administered by the City of Key West, which also maintains, via the city's tree commission, a small plant nursery there for raising trees and shrubs that adorn and shade public spaces throughout the city. Coogle said private citizens donated many of the trees and plants, engendering some quirky stories.

A beautiful silver buttonwood along the winding path is descended from a champion tree at the local golf course and was delivered via bicycle in 2004 from the Tampa nursery of arborist Patti Hoot-McCloud, who specializes in collecting and growing seeds from such trees. Also by the path hangs an enormous staghorn fern, a gift to the city of Key West from Cory Kulok, a dear friend of former city landscape inspector Tracy Kaufman. The fern was a wedding gift from Seminole tribe

Chief Dan Osceola and it had been passed down through generations of his family in the Everglades.

The former federal property was occupied by temporary housing during World War II and was deeded to the city in 1973, when Charles "Sonny" McCoy was mayor, hence the name. A flea market, among other oddities, was held there periodically for a couple of years and, in 1975, the area was designated a passive park with native plantings. The park was dedicated on Nov. 18, 1981, with speeches given by then-State Representative Joe Allen and Dr. Elton Gissendanner, executive director of the Florida Department of Natural Resources. It was a coconut farm for a while. Many of the palms on the South Roosevelt Boulevard bridle path are from there.

In 1990, the passive park designation was reinforced with a call for the addition of a wildlife pond and bird and butterfly garden. City landscaper at the time, Carl Weekley, developed the park's plan, working with landscape designer Kathy Wolf and with Fran Ford of the Florida Keys Audubon Society, a tireless advocate for the park. Although no formal butterfly garden exists, Coogle pointed out that many of the native plants in the park attract butterflies.

The freshwater wildlife pond in the back of the property was dug in 1992, with the $20,000 cost raised by private contributions and a challenge grant from Friends of Florida. The Toppino's donated the digging. To fill the pond's 206,000-gallon capacity, the fire department opened up a hydrant two blocks away and ran a big hose to the hole. Mrs. Ford brought in Australian Pat Boehm, an expert on natural pools (no chemicals), who advised on fish and plants for the pond, as well as Bob Ehrig, who helped design and planted the land surrounding the pond.

Coogle said the first fish to try the water, after the chlorine settled out, was a *Gambusia*, also known as a mosquito-eating fish. Then catfish, tilapia and mollies were added. It is turtle heaven for a thriving colony of red-eared sliders. Using materials from its own nursery there, the city installed food plants favored by birds and butterflies. Dragonflies zoom close to the surface. Resident, and migratory birds frequent the thriving wildlife habitat. An anhinga was recently seen on a tree branch by the pond, drying its wings in the morning sun. White-crowned pigeons love to eat the strongbark, ficus, blolly, gumbo limbo and *lignum vitae* fruits. Coogle said the wooden observation platform by the pond was built with money raised by the "Daughters of the Conch Republic," much of which was solicited, most appropriately, at local watering holes. During the winter season, the Audubon Society meets at the pavilion there every month, beginning each gathering with a bird walk.

Being so close to the Atlantic Ocean, the indigenous plants take a beating from storms that nearly always come from that direction. Coogle said the area was swamped five times in the 2004 hurricane season and four more times in 2005. Some trees toppled over after losing their footing in the saturated ground, but the native, thus salt-tolerant, *lignum vitaes*, buccaneer palms, Jamaican capers and many others, survived unscathed. Salt water contaminated the pond, which had to be drained, scraped and cleaned using an OMI "honey wagon" sucker truck, and refilled.

Indigenous Park is truly a local treasure not only because the plants are native, but also because the community came together to create it. Go take an evening stroll – the entrance to the path starts at the Key West Wildlife Center. Enjoy the ocean breezes, the greenery, the birds, and the peace.

Cynthia Edwards is a Key West Garden Club guest columnist. The former newspaper reporter and retired 16-year Key West Police Department Public Information Officer is now very active in the Garden Club.

A suspicious red-eared slider turtle checks out the photographer checking him out.

Photos by Lynne Bentley-Kemp

Cynthia Edwards with staghorn fern. a gift from Cory Kulok.

Additional Photographs

Rosi Ware, Reef Perkins & Sue Sullivan at the new officers induction ceremony

Kim Gordon at induction ceremony

Debbie Jo Clem, Annette Liggett, Sam Trophia, Jimmy Olson, Fran Ford, Roger McVeigh, & Mary Ann Westerlund planting Arbor Day trees.

Cynthia Domenech-Coogle busses Fran Ford

Scientific Names Index

Common Names Index